THE AG
INNOCENCE
3rd Edition

ISBN: 9781086774306

JOAN RILEY

Contents

List of Figures

This third edition is a black and white version of the 2nd edition that combines my two books "The age of Innocence" and Moving on (to a photo finish) into one volume. I have added an epilogue to bring the story up to date with a card from the Queen of England for our 60th Wedding anniversary and the unexpected results from my DNA ancestry that says I am related to someone on Coronation Street.

Acknowledgements

With special thanks to Leo, Gillian and Paul who gave me enough confidence (and help) to write these books. And also to Carol Arnall and people on the Amazon discussion site who informed and inspired me.

A special thank you to my colleagues at Granada who made the final picture as part of a card when I left.
Persona Granada (Sir Denis Forman) Granada coverage of President Kennedy shooting
Granada Television (The First Generation) Claude Watham on

Mike Parkinson's reaction to the Moors Murder tape.

Photograph courtesy of Joanna Lumley (The Avengers)
Photograph courtesy Granada TV (Programme on stress with Gordon Burns and Yoga teacher Penderil Reed.

Book 1: THE AGE OF INNOCENCE

This is an account of a young girl growing up in Gorton, Manchester between 1939 and 1948, taking in family scandals and domestic situations.

In a time before television, when access to a radio was determined by whether there was enough money to re-charge the accumulator, children and adults were far more innocent than today, with families closer.

This is the story of my life and family during and just after the Second World War.

Figure 1 Joan L Riley

GRANDDAD TOM

My Granddad Tom was a feisty, wiry man, built like a bantamweight boxer; and very dapper. On holiday with us at Butlins one year during a mini heat wave he never once appeared in public without waistcoat, jacket and tie.

After an accident at work on the railways he walked with a stick in a curious dot-and-carry-one motion and he had an elegant way of wiggling his stick before putting it firmly down on the ground. He used some of his scant compensation to buy a suitcase, which he filled with ladies' 'fancies' as he called them – ribbons, cottons, and pieces of lace, and for the bolder customer, even bloomers. He touted these around from door to door, and developed quite a nice little list of regulars, for he could certainly lay on the charm.

He was very proud of Mary, my Gran. She was a stately, elegant woman with a wide range of talents and was a wonderful cook. When retired she then took a job to help with the war effort making dinners for the directors of the Midland Bank in Spring Gardens, Manchester.

Although proud of his wife's cooking skills, Tom rarely ate anything except dry bread and almost mouldy cheese. It was his proud boast that he never ate butter, (until he suddenly developed a taste for it in his mid 90's) completely forgetting the fat used in Gran's delicious cakes, which he was often tempted to try. I could just imagine him in heaven saying "Well, I started to eat butter and looked what happened to me – I told you butter was bad for you."

On the other hand Gran hated at least two things about her husband; first his fierce temper, and the rows he had with their four sons about politics. Coming from Norfolk farming stock, Tom was a true blue Tory, but Uncles Jim, Charlie, George and my Dad Arthur were socialists ranging from the strongest red to watery pink. They seldom spoke to each other save to argue fiercely and volubly about politics.

It took only the smallest thing to set them off. Then Gran would sit, quietly seething until, calmly but lethally, she'd threaten to bang their heads together. In her prime after years of kneading dough, using a posser and turning a heavy mangle, she was well qualified to take anybody on.

Secondly Gran hated, loathed even, his teeth. Considering he always appeared well dressed this was one thing that let him down badly. Through constantly chomping on his pipe, he had worn his front teeth down to yellowish blackish stumps with two large Technicolor molars at the side. Gran swore she would do anything to stop him kissing her. "As soon as I see them pickle-stabbers coming towards me, I do a bunk into the kitchen."

Eventually he must have realised why his wife didn't feel amorous so to everyone's astonishment he decided to go to the dentist. This was to prove very traumatic for him <u>and</u> the poor dentist. In Granddad's own words he said "I sat in this 'ere chair and the dentist feller put a sort of mask on me face, some sort of ether I think it were.

"Well, it mustn't have taken properly because I remember seeing this 'ere face peering into me mouth and a grinding sound as me tooth was gripped and pulled. It hurt - I yelled - and knocked his tray of gewgaws up into t'air. I didn't know what I was doing and must have been waving my arms around because the dentist landed on the floor as well. I was shouting and shadow boxing and threatening to take on all-comers; being slightly dopey I thought I was being attacked. I certainly wasn't alone when I ran out of that surgery; most of t'others in the waiting room were in front of me. Damn noise must have put 'em off."

Granddad believed he had Viking blood and used as proof the remnants of ginger in his bushy moustache. I thought years of smoking thick twist tobacco had as much to do with the colour as his ancestors but it is thought that people with auburn hair need a stronger anaesthetic than normal so perhaps there was some truth in his belief.

Tom took great pride in the fact that the "silly bugger of a dentist never sent me a bill," and for a few years he managed to avoid another trip.

When the health service came into being, Tom, ever trying to get one over on "these damn Commies in t'Government", decided to go for some free treatment. The whole family went in fear and dread wondering what chaos he'd reap this time. Not to worry, he came back minus rainbow-coloured molars, singing the praises of the new dentist. "He thought just the same as me about the country going to the dogs. We had a lovely chinwag, put the world to rights we did. Fine man, just my type" he said.

Tom soon sported a gleaming white set of 'gnashers' as he called them and became even more popular with his 'ladies', even Gran.

Figure 2. Granddad Tom, Dad's Dad.

Photo taken several years later at my wedding.

Granddad's meanness was also legendary. Once and only once in living memory had he ever bought anyone anything? Usually Gran had to frog-march him to the shops and forcibly pull a hand, clenching a fistful of coppers, out of his pocket, to get him to pay for his own tobacco. That isn't to say that Gran was a spendthrift, at least not until she knew she was dying when she began to spend like a drunken sailor. They were brought up in times when money was very scarce and it was essential to watch your pennies.

After Granddad was "pensioned off", with insurance money for his injury, he decided to go into business for himself. He had been given what only he thought was generous compensation from the railway when something heavy had fallen on him from a great height, shattering his leg and making it, so the doctors said, highly unlikely he would ever work or walk properly again. He proved them wrong on both scores.

Reluctantly using some of his nest egg, he stocked up with enough ladies "knick-knacks" and luxuries to fill a small battered leather suitcase. Taking his case he would go hobbling from door to door hawking his wares and gradually he built up quite a nice little business for himself. He was quite a ladies man for he could be very charming when he wanted to be and business started booming. In fact he did so well that he decided to turn the parlour of their small terraced house into a shop.

Granddad was a very good craftsman and could make beautiful-looking furniture out of any sort of old wood. He scrounged old doors, tea chests and orange boxes, which he varnished to look like oak. His frugal ways extended to his painting for he used less than half the normal amount but still managed to get a perfect finish every time. It didn't take him long to fit out the front room with cupboards and shelves and his pride and joy, a lovely wooden counter. The whole effect looked extremely professional.

Their little haberdashery shop flourished for quite a few years before the slum clearance around Ardwick Green moved them to a corporation maisonette in Openshaw. Their new home had the advantage of hot water, bath and inside lav but there was no room for a shop, so sadly they had to go out of business.

Grandma used to buy some of the stock and served whenever she could, and as Granddad still kept his door-to-door trade, she was always kept quite busy. Indeed on the days when Granddad was away the ladies could come en-masse for their more 'personal' items. Granddad was very cheeky and embarrassed them when they asked for knickers or bust bodices; he was quite uninhibited and would openly display the most intimate garments, proudly pointing out their relevant qualities. Many were the not so maidenly blushes on the faces of the confused ladies. Although, according to Grandma, "There are some folk who encourage him. The hussies egg him on something dreadful", she'd say with a twinkle in her eye, for Gran was no prude.

The memorable day when Tom spent some money was when he insisted on going to the wholesalers himself. He came back with an armful of small parcels but wouldn't tell anyone what they were.

In fact he was so secretive about his purchases that Gran suspected he had found another woman on whom (unlikely though it was) he was lavishing presents. He had actually got another woman...me...his first Grandchild. I was about 16 to 18 months old at the time and never was a man so proud. He would bring all his drinking cronies in to watch me doing a little dancing jig on the top of the table; I had apparently started to do little dances almost as soon as I could walk, much to his delight.

He kept a close watch on his 'booty', barking at anyone who came near the packages. He waited until Mam and Dad came round on the Sunday, then, with a flourish, he brought out his treasures one by one. Proudly he opened first one and then the others. He took out a little underskirt, panties, socks, kid shoes, and then a beautiful little dress and a lovely bonnet. I had to be dressed up in them, have what they used to call 'have a fit' (I suppose this was short for a fitting), and then had to parade around giving a twirl here and a little dance there. I can vaguely remember even now the fuss this created. For years the family would talk about the day Dad had a brainstorm and spent some money. These clothes were for me to wear when he took me to his family home in Diss, in Norfolk to visit his mother; another surprise, for he rarely went back to his roots.

Although only a baby I can still remember things that happened then. Some of the memories may have been reinforced and altered by people talking about them over the years, but one memory was real because no one else knew about it.

I remember a very, very (to me) old lady, dressed in black with a funny bonnet on her head and smelling 'fusty'. This was my great Gran. She clutched me to her large, soft bosom and gave me a little present, something I treasured for years until it mysteriously disappeared. I learned later it was a gophering iron, but to me it was a fantastic toy, which I used to play with for hours on end. It was very small, about 3 inches long and made of iron and with a wooden handle. The back hinged open and you popped little coals inside the cavity to heat it up.

I thought the world of this little iron. And yes, I learned afterwards where it had gone it went the way of anything, which was not being worn or nailed down in our house...to Harry Crowe, the pawnbrokers. Whenever Mam was short of cash, and as our family grew larger, her visits to 'Uncles' became more frequent. Mam would collect articles together and tie them into a 'bundle'. These 'bundles' rarely ever saw the light of day again and were the source of quite a few heartaches to me over the years.

On one of the days at great Grandma's something happened, creating a memory so strong that it has stayed with me ever since. I was toddling down what seemed like a very, very long garden – being so small everything would have looked big to me. At the bottom of the path was a hedge of bushes with berries on them. On the other side three young boys were taking and eating the fruit off the bushes.

I remember that deep inside me I wasn't a little baby. I was a very cranky old person, I think a man. Furiously I tried to curse and order the boys away and frustratedly couldn't get the words out. I was really angry and couldn't understand why I hadn't got my stick to wave and thwack them with. Although angry with the boys I was even angrier with myself because I knew they didn't understand me and I couldn't get the words out I wanted to say. I was just jabbering so no one took any notice of me.

I don't have any explanation for the strong and vivid feeling I experienced other than reincarnation. Whatever it was it is a memory I've never forgotten. Inside I was a very different, nasty, ill-tempered person.

Granddad came from a place in Norfolk that was noted for the longevity of its inhabitants. Sadly he didn't reach his century, he just faded away and died but no one knew his exact age. He'd had a dispute with the pensions people when he reached (as he thought) 65. The baptismal records were the only sign that he'd existed and they showed his age as being two years less than he remembered. His explanation was that in those days, particularly in rural areas, parents had the habit of saving baptisms, christening two or three children together to save money. Obviously the christening date wouldn't be a true guide to the child's actual age. Anyway, he was in his late nineties when he died. He was a very remarkable man.

MONEY ON THE EMPTIES

We communicated conveniently through the wall between our kitchen and the Casson's. Mam and Mrs C had a series of knocks for 'I need to talk' or 'Don't answer the door the tally man/rent man is coming round'. Two knocks was my signal to run an errand, for which I was given a retainer of 6d rising through the years to 2 shillings a week. I used to fetch cigarettes, bottles of something or other and sometimes queue for silk stockings. Very welcome it was too, for sometimes I'd buy a comic, apple or sweets and at times I'd give Mam a much-needed sub, for she was always short of money.

Often we had no money for a radio accumulator battery so we'd put a jam jar against the wall in order to listen to 'Dick Barton, Special Agent', with Mrs C, knowing our situation and the fact that we all loved to listen to Dick Barton, thoughtfully turning up the volume so we could hear. It must have been a funny sight to see three or four kids with their ears glued to the wall

Mrs C, although a lot older than Mam, was a good friend and the two women always helped each other out. Mam was quite naive and learned a lot about worldly things from her neighbour. You see, as well as being a fountain of all knowledge, Mrs C worked as a layer-out for the local undertaker and many were the tales, funny and macabre, that she related to Mam.

At the time in question Mam had an evening job, between 6.0 and 9.0, cleaning at the brand-new Littlewoods store in Manchester. 'Posh' stores were unknown territory to Mam. Her treat was to browse around the shops in Cross Street, so the experience of working for a luxurious store such as this was, as she put it, "like fairyland".

She enjoyed her job very much and would come home telling of the wonderful things on sale and dreaming of what she would buy if Dad won the pools.

On one particular night Grandma Bond was baby-sitting. Gran heard the two knocks on the wall, and proud to be privy to our secret code, told me I was needed next door. I duly presented myself at the Casson's front door, which was opened by Leslie, Mrs C's 18-year-old son, who was seriously ill with consumption, an illness from which a number of the Casson family had died. Until he moved his bed to the parlour, we were kept awake at nights by the painful coughing fits, which the thin walls of our house did nothing to hide.

Leslie avoided my gaze and with his head bent down asked in a gruff voice, "Do you want to earn some money?"

Eagerly I said, "Yes" and he replied, "Go round to the shed".

I knew what he meant because I had noticed they had quite a few empties that needed to go back, and I started to plan which comic I'd buy with the money I got back on the bottles.

I scampered around the back, into the yard where a voice from inside the pitch-black shed whispered, "Come inside."

Completely innocently I went in.

I made out a dark shape, Leslie, who took hold of my hands and put something in them. At first, I thought it was a bottle but then the hairs on the back of my neck started to rise. It wasn't a bottle but something smooth, hard and warm.

Instinct told me this was wrong. Mam had warned us not to talk to strange men, and although Leslie wasn't strange, I realised this was what Mam had warned us about. Something bad was going to happen if I wasn't very careful. I was very, very frightened.

I tried to pull my hands away but Leslie held them together tightly with one hand. Then to my horror I felt the other hand scrambling round my legs trying to pull my knickers down.

"What are you doing? Stop it. Stop it. I'll tell me Mam if you don't stop". I started to cry very loudly.

"Oh don't be such a baby. Your friend Betty lets me. She doesn't cry, and stop making such a noise, you'll waken me Dad."

"Don't care about what Betty does, I'll scream and shout if you don't let go." I let out a sample scream which considering my fright was quite a good effort.

Pushing me out quite roughly he hissed "You silly girl. Go on you big baby."

Humiliated, I ran into the dirt square shared by the backs of houses in four streets. Although quiet and dark, the square held no fears. My fears weren't there. I kicked out so hard at a wall that I tumbled and cut my knee. Although I was only just nine, I still remember the rage I felt. All I could think was how dare he, who or what did he think I was.

Tears making dirt rivers down my face, muddied clothes and feet and a bleeding knee, I went home. Highly concerned, Gran comforted me, tut tutting, taking it for granted that I'd fallen.

Wise beyond my years, I didn't say anything. I just sobbed as Gran cleaned and mothered me. I cried myself to sleep that night and next morning told Mam all about it. She was absolutely horrified, her first reaction being "For heaven's sake don't tell your Dad or he'll kill him."

Her plea guaranteed silence, for Dad had a fierce temper and I thought "If he kills Leslie then he'll go to jail".

There was absolutely no chance of my saying anything to him.

Naturally, next morning, arms akimbo, Mrs C, Mam and Betty's mother grouped together in the back, discussed the matter. They talked to Betty, who said she'd pushed him away too. Later they confronted Leslie, who must have made very convincing excuses, considering what happened next.

I was very frightened every time I went to the Casson's to run an errand, because Leslie, whose bedroom I had to pass when I went through the front door, would whisper, "Do you want to earn some money"?

I would hold my breath as I rushed passed his door, terrified.

About a month later Mam told me I was going to the Saturday matinee with Leslie and his nephew Brian. "Oh no, I'm not. I'm not going anywhere with him".

I was quite determined about this. Mam who was normally a very easy-going woman was equally determined that I was going. "He wants to give you a treat to show that he's sorry and didn't mean any harm," she told me.

For three days I pleaded, terrified, begging Mam not to make me go, but she was adamant.

I considered telling Dad. I knew he would make sure I didn't go but reasoned that if he found out what had happened he might kill Leslie, for I'd been told he would. If he did he'd go to prison and they'd hang him. I thought long and hard about this, on the one hand hoping for Dad to kill this awful man, on the other not wanting any harm to come to Dad and worrying about how Mam would manage without his wage; she never had enough money even with them. In the end I realised that I'd have to go.

On the Saturday I wet my pants and was shaking with fright but Mam still propelled me to the Casson's front door where Leslie and Brian were waiting. We walked up the street, me dragging very reluctantly behind them. We crossed over Hyde Road and went into the Cinema. Leslie bought me a bag of chocolate éclairs, my very favourite sweets and an ice cream. I threw them all under the seat. I didn't want anything from HIM. Curled up tightly in a ball on the seat as far away from Leslie as I could get, I watched the screen seeing and hearing nothing of the film, just wishing I was back home.

Outside I muttered something about having to get back quickly and ran away from them across the main road, careless as to whether I was killed or not, and scurried down all the back streets to try to avoid them.

Breathless I arrived home and shut myself in our cold and sparsely furnished parlour, I cuddled in a corner until I'd calmed down thankful that I'd managed to get home safely. The cinema, sweets and ice cream were treats I seldom had, certainly not all at the same time but I felt somehow that I was being paid to keep quiet.

I will never ever know why Mam insisted I go with him. It was completely out of character for she was a wonderful, kind, considerate woman but I felt completely betrayed. I would still be interested to know just what excuse he had made.

THE EVACUEES

It started out just like any other school day, Friday the 1st of September 1939. I rolled out of bed and tottered down the narrow staircase. In the scullery, which nowadays would be called the kitchen, Mam had, as usual, put cold water (we had no hot water in our house) into the chipped white enamel bowl which stood in the long brown sink - I always thought this sink looked like a horse trough. As soon as she saw me, Mam poured a little hot water from the kettle into the bowl and I quickly splashed myself clean. The older children were left to wash themselves, but Mam would grab the younger ones and give them a good scrub with a flannel.

I then made a quick visit to the lavvy, a sort of hut outside in the back yard. There was nothing different there either. The splintered door still needed a coat of paint and the whitewash was peeling off the walls. Sheets of newspaper were, as usual, hastily pushed onto a nail at the back of the door. We imagined that only very rich people and public toilets had proper toilet paper and whenever I was given a penny to use one I would 'steal' sheets of the Jeyes paper to take home. It made very good tracing paper.

Breakfast was quite normal but with bigger helpings than usual; bread and jam for me, bread and dripping or condensed milk, which my brothers loved but I absolutely hated, and thick horrible porridge from which I was excused because it made me feel sick.

Thinking back there were two things that were slightly different. Mam had been crying and kept wiping her eyes on the bottom of her crossover pinny. Mam had a lot of problems, what with having four kids and very little money coming in, for Dad worked nights on the railways at that time and was very badly paid.

The other strange thing was that on a chair there were three brown paper parcels. Brown paper parcels weren't unusual because Mam used to wrap up bits of clothing and bedding and put them ready to take to the pawnshop (Uncles). The three parcels, however, were tightly tied with string; tied so tightly that their contents were bulging out, the string fastened into a large loop at the end. I started to suspect that something strange was going on when Mam took one of the parcels and put the loop around our Eric's head, the next one she put round George and the last one round mine.

"Come on then. Hurry up or we'll be late," she said. "Pick up your gas masks".

We put our gas masks, which were in cardboard boxes, round our shoulders and looked anxiously at Mam, wondering just what it was all about.

"You're going on a trip on a bus and a train, so come on. Hurry up. I shan't tell you again."

"But, but, What? Where?" we chorused, feeling quite excited but Mam just quietly ushered us gently out.

As we walked down the street Mam said very abruptly, "They are having a practice for the war so you're going away to the country for the weekend." We kids didn't really know what a war was. We'd heard that someone called Mussolini had a war with some place called Abyssinia and we used to sing a silly song about him "Oh what a surprise for El Duce. They do say he's had no spaghetti for weeks..."

We knew something was going to happen in England too because the only thing grown ups could talk about was a man called Hitler and someone called Chamberlain who was going to make sure there was no war. Although at one time we rarely saw an aeroplane, just lately there had been more of them. At one time, every time we heard a plane we would jump up and down pointing and screaming.... "Aira, aira, pom, pom, pom..." but lately we saw so many that we were getting tired of this game.

We trotted obediently behind Mam who was wheeling 12-month-old Jimmy in the old pram, which also carried our washing to the washhouse, and propelling Alan, who was nearly three. I wondered briefly what it was all about, but I wasn't very worried. Our only experience in those days was the adventure films we sometimes saw at the Saturday matinee. We would all sit mesmerised by the Lone Ranger and Tonto, Cowboys and Indians, Tarzan and Buck Rogers. They were always fighting someone or something and nothing really bad ever happened to them. Even when they were shot dead, you could be sure you'd see them again in some other film, so I didn't see why I should worry about a silly old war.

A row of charas (buses) was waiting near school and as we scrambled to get on them we were given labels to fasten onto our coats. Some of the kids were shouting with excitement, some crying, others screaming. All the mothers, however, were quiet and subdued, not their usual chatty selves at all.

The buses set off and in no time we arrived at Piccadilly Station. Here, we were guided to a platform quite near to the entrance where hundreds of children were already boarding a train. Mam ushered us into a compartment and stood watching through the window. Our Jimmy was held against her chest, asleep, whilst Alan clutched the bottom of her coat. Alan, the cherubic-looking terror of the family was for once very, very quiet. Seeing his brothers and sister going away must have been very upsetting for him.

The train moved off, and we squashed round the windows and waved and waved until we could no longer see the station or the mothers, then we sat down and patiently waited to see what was going to happen next.

First of all we were given a tin, which we were told contained 'iron rations'. These tins were for emergency use only and, we were severely warned, mustn't be opened without permission. The small tin boxes were sealed all round the edge with adhesive tape - something like Elastoplast. We pretty soon realised that you could peel this tape carefully off, open the tins, and sneak out a little corner of one of the chocolate bars inside, resealing the box afterwards.

There must have been more than chocolate in the box but that is all I remember, for even before the war, chocolate was a great treat for us. It wasn't very long before most of the children were carrying empty tins around with them.

Eventually the train pulled into a station, which we later learned was Hazel Grove. We didn't see any signs to tell us where we were. I think they had already started taking signs away (to confuse any German paratroopers who might land in England).

I suppose we were given something to eat and drink but I don't remember what or when. I do remember, though, that we were herded into lines and the 'nit' nurse inspected us. We knew we were clean because our Mam looked through our hair every week before it was washed - she called it 'chatting'.

Just one girl was taken out of line and we knew what that meant. She would have her hair washed in evil smelling liquid that everyone could smell a mile off. If she was badly infected she'd have her hair cropped very, very short, and sometimes even shaved. We felt sorry for her - but we needn't have worried because she was looked after by one of the teachers, the most elegant and beautiful, and the only teacher who had a car. From then on she sported a very stylish haircut and very stylish clothes too.

After the 'nit inspection' we were shepherded into groups by WVS ladies carrying lists of names of families willing to take evacuees. The ladies stopped here and there to select a child who was the right age and sex for someone on their list. The chosen ones were shepherded onto one of the buses.

Most of the buses had filled up and gone, and we three were among the last to be chosen. Two of the ladies held a serious conversation before directing us to the last bus. It was rather worrying...

One by one, or two by two, someone either met the children on our bus as the bus stopped, or were taken into a house by the efficient looking ladies who would then tick their names off the list. When it came to our turn there was only one other girl left on the bus.

The bus stopped in Mill Lane and our WVS lady got off the bus and knocked on one of the doors. The conversation didn't look very promising because the lady of the house kept shaking her head. She then walked up to the bus, looked at us but still shook her head. I started fretting - what was the matter with us? Had someone told them we were naughty? Well we were, sometimes, but not as bad as some of the children who'd been chosen at the beginning. Did they think we were dirty and scruffy? Well, at least we didn't have nits and Mam always kept us as clean as she could.

By this time it was getting late, Eric was sobbing, George was aggressive and kept nudging me in the ribs so, of course, I had to nudge him back. We were all close to tears and tired, and our WVS ladies were looking very anxious.

The commotion must have disturbed another lady who came out of her bungalow. She was a very motherly looking lady, plump with white hair and rosy cheeks. She was joined by another, even older lady with even rosier cheeks. The two kept wiping their eyes on crisp white handkerchiefs; they held a whispered conversation, nodded, smiled and then pointed to another bungalow, Hawarden, in the little cul-de-sac just off Mill Lane.

The WVS lady knocked on the door and after a while came out with another lady; they were smiling. But the lady with them, Mrs Bowden, didn't look very happy.

There was nothing sinister about what happened. There was nothing wrong with us. I later found out that it had been difficult to place three children, of different sexes, and the authorities were trying to find a place where we could be together.

The lady who had turned us down so emphatically had wanted boys, and then changed her mind about having any children at all. As things turned out it was a good thing the lady hadn't wanted us for her son could have been a problem for me.

He was about 13 and went to Stockport Grammar School and became good friends with my brothers and they really thought a lot about him, because he was so much older they looked up to him.

One day Eric brought me a note from him, it read something like "If you let me f... you I will give your brothers my Boys' Own books and a pair of roller skates". I was furious and somehow knew what he meant. I shook my fists at him as I stood at the garden gate and then realised I had the problem of getting rid of the letter. What to do with it? I ripped it into tiny pieces and buried then and the 'rude' words I chewed and swallowed, fearful that the Bowdens would find it!

All things considered I think that George and Eric had the easiest and most enjoyable time. They were staying with the Coopers, and their elderly mother. They were the kindest people in the world. Mrs C and her mother were so sweet and, well, motherly that the boys really had landed in clover. The Coopers were in their late fifties and had never had children of their own. They idolised the boys, particularly Eric, who at five was a very lovable and well-mannered child.

I was I believe taken under sufferance by the Bowden's who had a small daughter, Nora, and lived in a bungalow just across the small cul-de-sac. About a year afterwards Mrs Bowden had a new little girl. Although they always tried to make me feel welcome the new arrival made me feel I was more in the way than ever.

I never felt really at home in the bungalow. I know I should have because it had all the luxuries we didn't have at home, luxuries such as a room of my own, hot water, a bath and an inside toilet. There was a dressing table, wardrobe and chest of drawers; things I'd hardly seen before, except at Gran's, for she had an old wardrobe and a chest of drawers. At home our clothes, such as we had, hung on nails behind bedroom room doors, or in the hall. There were proper bedclothes too – blankets and sheets; mostly we used old coats and the peg rugs Granddad made were put on our beds.

For all its comforts, I was always frightened in that room. Perhaps it was being in a strange place, or being on my own but the painting of a group of cherubs hovering in flight disturbed me the most. The eyes in the painting were so realistic that I felt they were watching me, following me around the room. It was very scary and I would dash into the room, jump quickly into bed, covering myself right up to my nose with bedclothes and keeping my eyes tightly shut so that I couldn't see the angels.

Although Mrs. Bowden was fairly kind, she looked and was quite stern. This austere look was reinforced by the fact that she was, to me, very tall and thin, her black hair severely pulled back into a bun. She had very sharp features, a long thin nose and was usually dressed in a long skirt and with a high-necked blouse. Her habit of suddenly going to the piano and singing in a very high soprano voice always startled me. She usually burst into songs like 'Come into the garden, Maude,' or 'Your tiny hand is frozen.' Never had I heard such a shrill voice. Never had I been used to mothers who had time to play the piano and sing at the drop of a hat, and this habit did nothing to endear me to her. If I were concentrating on something else, her sudden outbursts would make me jump and made me even more wary.

I also had feelings of resentment over the monthly sweet ration. Mrs. Bowden would put Nora's and mine together into a tin and dish out a sweet or a piece of chocolate to each of us. Because the tin seemed emptier every time she opened it, I concluded that either Mrs B was helping herself to our sweets or that Nora was getting my share as well as hers whilst I was at school.

It was a beautiful autumn and we children would spend all day playing in the fields but my idyll was first broken in October, just over a month after I was evacuated. A letter came in the post as we were having breakfast. Mrs. Bowden opened it, read it and told me that I had a new baby sister. At first I was very excited and pleased at the idea of another girl in the family, another girl to play with and dress up. Just like a doll I thought, until... Mrs B started to tease me saying "Your nose is certainly going to be pushed out of joint now. Mark my words, your sister will be the one to get all the attention. I bet your Dad and Granddad spoil her instead of you".

I went cold and felt physically sick. Did this mean that my Mam and Dad wouldn't want me anymore? Would I have to stay with the Bowden's for ever and ever? I ran into the garden and hugged myself to try to get a little comfort. Any letters written by Mam and Dad were I think addressed to Mrs. Bowden. I don't think I got any addressed personally to me and if I had I know Mrs. Bowden would have opened them first anyway. All the news I had been given was that Mam had been evacuated to Blackpool with Alan and Jimmy and now, of course, she was with my little sister, Rita, too. It was awful not having any proper news of them, not being able to reassure myself that I was still wanted.

After crying myself to sleep secretly for a couple of nights, I reasoned that having a sister wouldn't make much difference. I knew for certain deep inside that when the war was over Mam and Dad would come to collect me some day. I waited and waited but the war went on an awful long time.

I really missed Mam and Dad and my brothers and another thing I missed was Mam and her weekly 'nit hunt'. I worried and worried and imagined every itch to be a head full of creepy crawlies. It got to such a pitch that after Christmas I hoarded a sixpence I had been given instead of putting it in my moneybox. I went to the top of Mill Lane to the chemist shop and bought a fine toothcomb and a bottle of natural coloured nail polish. When everywhere was quiet I'd put a paper on the floor and combed and combed my hair, looking for nits or anything crawling. Apart from a few stray bits of dandruff, there was nothing. I knew it was dandruff because Mam had told us that you pressed whatever you found between your two thumbs. If it popped then it was a nit. The nail polish I painted on, hoping that no one would notice. It looked very pretty and I was so proud, but kept hiding my nails every time Mrs B looked at me.

So, having taken precautions, I felt quite confident when the nit nurse arrived at school. We stood in line and one by one the nurse inspected us and then said, "Right, you go and sit down".

When it was my turn she didn't tell me to sit down but motioned me to one side whilst she continued her inspection. I really panicked then. Oh no, the comb hadn't worked I had livestock in my hair. Panic set in. When she'd finished the inspection she asked me "When did you last wash your neck?"

Surprised, I answered "This morning, Miss".

In a very snooty voice she replied, "Rubbish. Dear me. No you did not, not for a good few mornings I'd say. It's filthy. A nice girl like you shouldn't have such a dirty neck. Don't ever come to school like that again."

Utter relief... I didn't have nits, just a dirty neck. No shame at all for being shown up in front of the class for having a dirty neck, just relief I had no livestock.

For a time I was I suppose quite content. The weather was mostly beautiful, very sunny and warm in the spring and summer, although it could be quite cold in the winter with lots of snow. Apart from the fact that we were separated from our Mam we were really having a lovely time, running wild and making full use of the fields, woods and stream that ran at the back of the bungalows. We chased cows and loved to jump on the sun-hardened cowpats to try to break them. We picked wild flowers and loved to sniff the wild garlic.

Suddenly it seemed years and years since I had last seen my mother, father, brothers - and I had never seen my little sister Rita. Actually it was about 18 months that Eric, George and I had been evacuated to Hazel Grove. Now although Hazel Grove seemed to us to be the other end of the country, in actual fact it was a mere 10 to 12 miles from our home in Gorton. To the three of us, kids of five, seven and nine when we were first evacuated, it was as though we had been parted for ever both in time and distance.

One day I just couldn't bear it any longer. Using the handle of a spoon I managed to push two sixpenny pieces out of the slot of my moneybox. My heart beating madly, I tied one or two things into a brown paper parcel; the bottle of nail varnish, my nit comb, three toffees I had saved from the ones Mrs. Bowden had given to me, an apple and a spare pair of black school knickers.

When the coast was clear and the family had gone to the shops, I sneaked out of the house. I had no idea where to catch the trolley bus home. Then I remembered that buses to Reddish went from the 'Rising Sun' pub corner. I caught a trolley bus, paid my fare out of one of the sixpences and very soon the bus reached the terminus. I remembered Reddish because we had been to Debdale Park quite a few times, so I knew where to get the next bus. Within a couple of minutes I was getting off the bus at Cross Street.

Figure 4 The junction of Cross Lane, Wellington Street and Cross Street,

Well, that part had been fairly easy but the worst was to come. What would I say to my Mam and Dad? Would they send me back? How would I face the Bowdens after this? What if Dad was in a fierce mood and hit me? I don't ever remember him hitting me but I was terrified of his loud roar and temper. Panic gripped me and I trudged slowly down the road home, desperate to put off the fateful moment when I would have to face the family.

By this time, my mother had come back from Blackpool. This much I had learned from letters that Mrs. Bowden sometimes read out to me.

I would have known Mam was in anyway because the front door was, as usual ajar, kept open with an old flat iron. I walked down the lobby, into the kitchen and surprised a startled Mam who was giving Rita, my new sister, milk and a rusk. Rita was by this time 17 months old. At first Mam was lost for words, she was too surprised. Then she grabbed me and gave me a cuddle - cuddles were quite rare in our family and it felt strange but good to be squeezed like that.

"What? Why? How"? Mam managed finally managed to blurt out.

"I've run away Mam. I thought I was never going to see you all again. So I just took some money and ran away."

"Well, I never did" Mam spluttered. "We'll have to wake your Dad up and see what he has to say."

Now, when Dad was on nights it was an absolute rule, to be broken only on pain of the threat of a good hiding, not to wake Dad. "Oh", I wailed. "Don't wake him. Can't you wait till he gets up Mam"?
"No" she replied quite forcefully, "We've got to tell him NOW."

Tell him she did, Dad was just as flummoxed as she was and didn't know what to do or say. It never dawned on me that the Bowdens would be worried about where I was. And to this day I still don't know how word was got to them that I was safe at home.

I never saw the Bowdens again. The only time I heard about them was from Eric. He stayed with the Coopers for another year, for he was very happy there. They spoilt him and cosseted him and wanted to adopt him but Mam wouldn't hear of it. George had already moved out of the Coopers bungalow because two boys had proved to be hard for them to manage. He lived in another house and was quite happy. He learnt how to darn socks, a very unusual hobby for a boy, and he went back home shortly after me.

Eric told me that Mr Bowden had been taken ill with Hodgkinson's disease and had died. I felt shame and guilt. I should have sent them a Christmas card or something because they had for 18 months been very kind to me. Any problems were mostly my fault and it must have been strange to them to have a nine-year-old suddenly thrust upon them.

Figure 5 The Bonds

OUR 'BACK'

Nothing ever grew on the large square patch of dirt at the back of our houses; no grass, no weeds, just puddles when it rained and dog dirt. This didn't stay there for long because some eagle-eyed woman would bustle out, waving a shovel and grumbling all the while about having to get rid of the mess.

The square, formed by the back yards of terraced house from the four streets surrounding it, had once been the site of back-to-backhouses, long since demolished. It was our pride and joy, for none of the other streets enjoyed the luxury of a communal meeting place; a large patch almost the size of a football pitch which was used as a meeting ground, playing field, somewhere to have street parties and bonfires and, oh, a million things.

During the war, and for years afterwards, a large brick air-raid shelter was built just outside our back yard. This gave another bit of status to us for when the sirens sounded we would all have jolly get-togethers. Cosily squashed together, some of us on bunks, others squatting on chairs or on the floor, we shared 'goodies' and sang songs, some of them quite daringly rude to childish ears. For years afterwards I would sing, 'With her head tucked underneath her arm, she walked the bloooody tower... at the midnight ooower.' The lengthened vowels gave a ghostly sound to the words. We had a habit, too, of saying 'Bloody' and when given a telling-off for swearing, would innocently reply that "We were only singing that song about the Queen with no head."

It was hardly surprising that nothing grew on this busy thoroughfare. Kids, and there were quite a lot of them, played and fought there, prams were positioned outside back gates whilst mothers hung out sheets or banged dirt out from coconut-matting 'carpets' that squared almost every floor. These rough carpets looked reasonably clean on the surface, and had bright patterns, the problem being that dirt collected underneath. If they weren't lifted and brushed regularly there would be an extra covering of dirt looking just like a negative of the top carpet. Of course carpet-bashing days were never on the same days as washing day, for woe betide anyone who knocked dust around when the Oxydol-white clothes were on the lines.

When she left school, in 1920/21, Mam got a job in the laundry at the Midland Hotel in Manchester. This was a very hard, extremely hot job for a young girl but it **was** in the Midland, one of the top hotels. An extremely hard worker, Mam soon made her way up the ranks of the laundry and finished as a Hoffman Presser before she got married.

Her experience must have stayed with her all her life because she prided herself on having the whitest whites and the cleanest colours. This she achieved by using the public washhouse. On Hyde Road, Gorton on the opposite side but very near to Belle Vue, there was a large imposing building which housed the public swimming baths with the washhouse and wash baths at the side of it. Mam had a regular booking for the same time every week: two hours, which she had to make sure she re-booked every week because some of the times were very popular and soon taken up if you forgot to book.

Almost all the women we knew used these Municipal Wash-houses, which were part of Gorton Baths. In a strange way this weekly washday was also a chance to get together with the same group of mothers and have a bit of a gossip, although the noise made this quite difficult but they still managed somehow.

Occasionally I helped Mam with the wash, (I suspect I was smuggled in because I don't think you were allowed to bring helpers in, although when older I did the wash by myself a few times) but my goodness those washhouses were warm: it was a bit like having a sauna with all your clothes on. The first hurdle you had to make was trundling our old pram, (well used, particularly after the 8th baby) which was filled to overflowing with clothes, down Church Lane (later called Cambert Lane) and down Hyde Road to the washhouse. The pram was very heavy to push and moved sideways unless you controlled it: just think of a supermarket trolley filled with the washing for 9 or 10 people and you'll have some idea of how difficult it was to push. If Mam had forgotten to oil the wheels, which often happened, then it would it squeak all the way down the road announcing our intentions to everyone around.

Once inside we went to our allotted 'station' where Mam put all the 'whites' into the large boiler at the side of our place, put powder in – it was probably Rinso or Oxydol- then set the boiler going and watched with satisfaction as the clothes churned around and the steam puffed out. Then the stainless steel sink at the other side of our 'station' was filled with hot water and more washing powder and Mam started to pummel and scrub the coloured clothes before putting them in an adjacent sink to rinse. By the time she had finished the coloureds the whites would be ready and were then put onto the very hot rails, which came out of the walls, and when pushed back in dried the clothes. Same with the coloureds and at the end of the two hours we were left with a neat pile of beautifully clean clothes that we had to trundle back home to be ironed, although if folded properly a lot of the clothes didn't have any creases to take out. If Mam was lucky enough to get an extra session she would take in neighbours washing and the coppers she got for this helped to supplement her frugal budget.

THE MONEY MAKER

It's an arguable fact that people with good strong noses, or to put it bluntly, large noses, often have a flair for making money.

Most of our family are sadly lacking, both in the nose and the moneymaking departments. That is with the exception of our George who has been blessed on both counts, although it has to be admitted his money making has been rather erratic.

He started looking for ways of becoming rich when he was quite small. One of his first ideas was getting his friends to help him make a 'bogie'. They knocked together a rather rickety box and fixed it onto two pram wheels, with two handles jutting out at the front.

Mrs Casson, our next-door neighbour, had a dog. His name is now politically incorrect so I shall have to call him Dusty. A black Labrador-type with 57 varieties of ancestors, he was a big, lumbering dog, daft as a brush and very easy going. George harnessed him to the bogie with ropes and leads and charged the smaller children a ha'penny each for the privilege of trotting sedately round our 'back'. (This was the dirt-covered area, which separated four sets of terraced houses and formed a large square at the back of each.)

The bigger boys, seeing this, wanted a ride as well. George certainly wasn't going to take two of them for a penny and the boys certainly wouldn't pay a penny each, so four of the big lads squashed into the cart.

Naturally they weren't content to stroll around but got Dusty to go first from a trot to a canter then a gallop. Round and round, faster and faster they went until inevitably the bogie collapsed, the boys were flung out and poor Dusty careered on dragging the wheels behind him until he finally came to a stop.

Mrs Casson was not amused and threatened George with hell fire and damnation but he soon bounced back with another idea; hens. He started out with three – Snowball, Brownie and Vera. The first two names were self-explanatory but Vera? I've no idea why. They became part of the family and although they had a sort of Heath Robinson type coop in our yard, they roamed free, and if the back door was left open they roamed around our scullery too.

In the scullery we had one of those kitchen cabinets which were very popular during the war, green and cream with sliding glass doors at the top, and a door which hinged down to make a table top. Mam had put butter and jam onto the top ready to make jam butties for our tea, when she found she was running short of bread. She nipped out to the local shop, which was only two houses and an entry along from ours, so she wouldn't have been gone very long.

She came back to face what looked like a massacre with everywhere covered in what seemed like greasy blood. Looking further she discovered one of the hens on the top of the cabinet, pecking away at the butter, her head and feet covered in jam with jammy prints all over the place. The other hens, feathers covered in the sticky gungy mess, strutted around the scullery looking very proud of themselves, and leaving evidence of their crime all over the place.

Mam was not best pleased at losing all her butter ration for the week, not to mention the jam, and said that either the hens went or she did. What made it worse was that normally she sold our butter to make ends meet and we usually had to make do with margarine, which in those days was horrible. I found it uneatable but my six brothers would eat anything so it was no hardship for them. This was one of the few occasions when she had allowed herself the luxury of butter. She had often asked George to get rid of the blessed hens but this time she really meant it. George took her seriously this time, for it wasn't often our easy going Mam lost her temper.

He had made friends with a man on the local allotment, and was already negotiating to build hencoops there with the view to expanding his hens and his empire.

He got a posse of boys to walk Indian-file down to the allotment carrying an assortment of boxes, wood, hens, and hen food. They deposited themselves and the hens at the allotment where the kind man helped them all to build new homes for the chickens.

This proved very successful; George sold his eggs, bought more hens and finished up as one of the darlings of the neighbourhood. All the ladies who baked vied with each other for his new laid eggs. Eggs were not easy to come by then and new-laid ones almost impossible. He was tempted with offers of slices of home-made cakes, fairy buns and over-the-top prices for his booty, which the ladies reckoned made their cakes light as a feather. He was certainly a happy, and was soon to become a 'bonny' lad.

When he was fourteen he made friends with a boy of the same age. He was very tall and thin and his father had a few butchers' shops in the area. This boy took a liking to me and used to follow me around. If I was going to the pictures he would do his best to follow me but I would take all sorts of detours to evade him.
This boy, I'll call him Brian but that wasn't his name, and George would work weekends in one of the shops, learning the trade. When the boys left school, which they did at fourteen, Brian's father employed them both in one of his shops and later when he thought they had acquired enough experience, he bought a small shop for Brian and the idea was that he and George would run it together.

Naturally having a shop of their own with all the help they needed and a good supply of ready-cut meat ready to sell to eager customers as part of their rations, was the boys' idea of heaven.

Oh thank goodness. Dad was smiling now. "Which school would you like to go to?" he asked.

"I don't know anything about any schools, Dad. You pick one for me."

"Right then, I'll put down Fairfield High School. That used to be The Moravian College for Young Ladies and I think it will have to be a good school to turn you into a young lady my girl. Is that all right with you?"

I nodded, still mesmerised with the news and still not understanding what it was all about.

Mam and me were the only people who weren't surprised to learn I'd passed my scholarship. We weren't surprised because neither of us knew what it was all about. I'd done a test at school and now was going to a new school. So what? My Dad was more worldly and was surprised but pleased, but the person who showed the most astonishment was Miss Green, the headmistress at St James' C of E school in Gorton.
Standing on the platform at assembly she started to read out names of people who were going to other schools. My name "B" was the second to be called. Miss Green, a stately lady with a distinctive hairstyle – two long coils twisted round and round her ears, just like large headphones, had, I thought, a formidable manner. She looked at her list and appeared not to believe what she saw, for she took off her spectacles and cleaned them before proceeding.

"Joan Bond", she stuttered, a look of complete amazement on her face. "Joan Bond, Joan Bond...Fairfield High School?"

Because Dad had a poorly paid job and seven, almost eight, children, I was entitled to free everything...transport, meals, books, uniform. We soon received a letter with instructions on what to get and where to go and a voucher to pay for them.

Mam, who's idea of 'up market' shopping was to go to Cross Street instead of the market, was terrified at the thought of actually going to St Anne's Square in Manchester. Why, she had never ever been to Deansgate, or King Street, never looked in Kendal's window. These places were not for the likes of us.

She put off the fateful day as long as she could but eventually had to get my uniform.

We walked up and down outside Henry Barrie, school outfitters, in St Anne's Square until she plucked up courage to go inside. We were greeted by a very distinguished looking man, who took the 'chitty' off Mam and said, in a cultured voice. "Come this way, please, I know just what Modom needs".

His perfect vowels did nothing for Mam's composure and blushing and trembling she followed him to another counter.

When I quickly told her the whole sorry story, the old lady from next door, didn't need to be asked twice, she'd been down that road herself. She pressed a coin into my hand. "Think on my girl, look sharpish, we don't want your Mam getting into trouble now, do we?"

Because it wasn't a Monday when the pawnshop was full of women queuing to put items in, or a Friday when some of the same women were getting them out again, the shop was thankfully empty.

Out of breath, I handed the ticket and money over the counter to the pawnbroker. "Hello m'love" he said, "And where's your mother today then?" The pawnbroker knew our family well because Mam was quite a good customer.

"Oh I can run the fastest so she sent me. Me Dad's going for a new job this afternoon and Mam says if he finds out where his suit is he'll skin her alive."

"Dear, dear me" said Harry Crowe; for that's what we called him although I never found out if it was indeed his name. "Can't have that now, can we?" Taking a suit off a hangar, he carefully folded it and placed it in my arms. Then handing me back a sixpence, said "Tell your mother I'll not charge her interest this time as it's important."

I pushed the coin down into my sock and ran back home. Mam was waiting for me at our back yard gate and dashed inside with the suit. The trousers were quickly folded onto the makeshift ironing board made out of old blankets and towels put on the end of the table. She spat on the iron and started to press down on a sopping wet cloth. The kitchen was shrouded in steam when Dad came downstairs a few minutes later.

"I thought I'd come down for a wash to save time later" he said. "Oh I see you found it then", he nodded towards the suit. Turning to me he asked, "And what have you been up to my girl, sitting there with a red face looking all guilty like?"

I gulped on a spoonful of soup. "Er, nothing Dad, I'm just trying to eat as fast as I can and this soup's really hot. I don't want to be late back to school."
I called in on the outside lav on my way back and carefully tied the sixpence in the corner of a handkerchief, which I pushed underneath the elastic in my knicker leg.

All afternoon I daydreamed about what comics I'd buy. Not the Beano or Dandy. We usually got them, weeks old, dog-eared and ripped, but still readable – just – from uncle Alf's barber shop. No, I'd get a 'Film Fun' or 'Sunny Stories' and, yes, I'd get an apple too.

As usual I called in the library that was directly opposite St James' School. This was one of my favourite places and I'd spend hours looking through the adult section, deciding which books I'd take out when I got my adult ticket. My favourite that time was 'The Whiteoaks of Jalna' by Mazo de la Roche, a family saga that went into quite a few volumes. I usually managed to get though a few pages before the librarian came creeping up on me, forfeited the book and gave me a real ticking off, but today she was otherwise engaged so I spent longer than ever reading.

Mam was looking rather flustered when I got in. "Oh you're late. Been in the library again, have you?" I nodded.

"Well, I don't know what we'll have for us tea. I've run out of potatoes and I'm skint. You'll just have to have toast and dripping and the lads can have condensed milk butties."

I cringed at the idea. I hated dripping butties, unless they had the jelly from the bottom and I knew that had gone into the soup. As for condensed milk, "Uggh, my brothers would eat anything" I thought.

I pulled out my scruffy hankie and handed it to Mam. "Here, I couldn't give it to you before 'cos Dad was there. Harry Crowe said he'd not charge interest this time, as it was 'portant."

Mam untied the hankie, muttering about how this was a real piece of luck. "Here, go and get three pennorth of chips and ask if they have some scratching? We can have chip butties for our tea now."

Chip butties with plenty of salt and vinegar and, if we were lucky, scratchings from the fish batter, too, were my favourite. I'd rather have that than some manky old comics any day.

Figure 6 Me, Joan Bond in 1945

UNCLES

Our Mam had a very good relationship with Uncle; she visited him at least twice a week. And no, I don't mean she had lovers; the Uncle I'm talking about was Harry Crowe, the pawnbroker on Hyde Road, Gorton.

His was a very popular place. Every Monday morning there would be a large queue of women waiting to "pop" their bits and pieces and every Friday a trickle of these self-same women trailing along to redeem some of them.

In retrospect the pawnbroker had two very distinct sides. On the one hand he was a moneylender who charged a quite extortionate rate of interest. For instance my mother would pawn Dad's suit on Monday and get perhaps a shilling or two in exchange (this could vary depending on the mood 'Uncle' was in). On Friday it cost Mam about 1s/3p or more to get it out again. Not a bad return for five days interest.

On the other hand 'Uncle' would take in bundles and give a few coppers, perhaps up to a sixpence back on them. These consisted mostly of old clothes and bedding wrapped with brown paper and string or sometimes tied up in a shirt.

Mam had quite a racket going in this respect. She would trawl round jumble sales and pick up a handful of clothes for a couple of pence. She sometimes came back with really elegant 30's type dresses. You know, the ones cut on the bias, very flattering. I loved to dress up in these although they were far too old for me. I'd stuff socks into one of Marjorie Birtwell's old bras and parade around the house feeling quite glamorous. They would, however, eventually find their way into Harry Crowe's. Mam was making a few coppers profit from these for they were seldom ever redeemed.

I could not imagine how the pawnshop made any money on the bundles because there they would lie, looking very forlorn, gathering dust, and stacked high on shelves until their time was up (they were kept for about a year) and then would go, only pawnbrokers knew where, never to be seen again.

Unfortunately jumble sales are usually seasonal and in the fallow period Mam would pawn anything that didn't move. I lost quite a few of my 'treasures' that way. And then one unforgettable Monday morning she pawned my school blouses by mistake. Monday morning was a very busy time for my mother. She had to go to the pawnshop quite early in order to get coppers hopefully to last her for most of the week, for food and my bus fare.

All the money she got was accounted for and there was absolutely no chance of seeing my blouses again until Friday. When I realised what she had done I was absolutely devastated and cried and shouted, but it was no use. "You'll have to wear one of our George's shirts," said Mam, trying to be helpful. All our clothes, no matter how shabby, were beautifully cleaned and ironed so the shirt was quite respectable.

The problem was the shirt had a collar. I had passed a scholarship to go to Fairfield High School, which was classed as quite a good school. It had previously been The Moravian College for Young Ladies – the Moravians being people who valued education, even for girls, at a time when this was unusual. The ethics of the school still existed and we were supposed to behave at all times like young ladies. Always wear a hat and gloves, never eat in the street and act always with decorum.

Our uniform blouses were square necked, the edges showing about three inches above the square necks of our gymslips and looked very smart, so a blouse with a collar stood out like a sore thumb.

Furtively I edged my way into the hall for the morning's assembly and positioned myself behind a very large girl in the hope that I wouldn't be seen. No way. Headmistress Miss Bradley spotted me straight away. I could feel her eyes staring in my direction. As soon as morning prayers were over and before the school's daily announcements were read, the formidable woman commanded "You girl, the girl out of uniform" and pointed in my direction. By this time I was bending down peering up from behind the girl in front. The girls around moved to expose me. "Yes, you there. Come up here."

Now Miss Bradley, a full-bosomed lady usually dressed in twin sets, pearls and tweed skirts, had the prime position in the middle of the platform. Here she would sit, arms akimbo and brogue-shod feet placed firmly on the floor, legs slightly apart.

This afforded people below a full view of the lady's directoire knickers. Elastic delicately placed round each plump lisle-covered-knee. I marvelled at the number of pairs she owned. Every day it would be a different colour – white, pink, green, blue, or puce.

The walk down the hall couldn't have been worse if I'd been going to the gallows. I shuffled along, being chided all the while to "Hurry up".

The only thing that was keeping me going was thinking about those colourful knickers. Which colour did I like best, the green? No, I think I liked the pink best, and I had decided on the blue when I reached the stage steps, putting off the fateful moment as long as I could.

A small, young-for-my-age 12 year old, I climbed up the steps and arrived on the platform where I was beckoned to the front. We must have looked a very strange pair; the large buxom head and the scrawny little schoolgirl. I could see that all the teachers were staring at me and out of the corner of my eye I noticed the geography teacher, not noted for her dress sense, giving me a sympathetic look. Probably she, too, had suffered from the Head's perfectionism while hundreds of my fellow pupils were watching me curiously from below.

"Well", Miss B fired questions at me. "Why are you out of uniform? What on earth is that you are wearing? Where is your regulation school blouse?"

She fingered the collar on the shirt and gave a little mooey of disgust. "You are a disgrace to the school. I will not have girls arriving at this school in such a state of undress. We have standards to keep up, as you very well know."

I should have told her "My mother's pawned them, or 'popped' them", and can imagine the shock that would have caused. Although most of the girls wouldn't have known what I was talking about it would have shaken the Head out of her pomposity and made her lost for words for once. Alas, I wasn't confident enough to be truthful.

I made a very big mistake when I replied "Sorry Miss Bradley but my mother hasn't ironed it."

She gave me a withering look of scorn. "You lazy, lazy girl. Why didn't you iron it yourself?" she said.

Red-faced, I mumbled something like, "I didn't have time."

Miss B harrumphed "Well, you must wear your science overall all day and cover yourself up. Make sure it's buttoned all the way down. I wouldn't like anybody to see one of my girls dressed that way, and be sure you are dressed correctly tomorrow."

The overall was black and made me look even thinner than I was, and I had to wear it all week. I had, of course, got quite a reputation by now and spent the whole week dodging round corridors trying to hide away. Strangely, no-one mentioned that I should only be wearing the horrible overall for one day.

News must have got to the Headmistress that I came from a large poor family and I like to think she was making a kind of apology to me when I was summoned to her study a few weeks later.

Naturally when I got the call I was terrified wondering what I'd done wrong. The only other time I'd been in her study was when I went with my mother for an interview before I started at the school. My dealings with the lady had been when she passed me in a corridor and invariably chastised me for untidy hair.

"Put it in bunches" she'd say, and when it was in bunches "It's still untidy – plait it", or "Tie it back".

I have the kind of hair that usually looks untidy and can stick out all over the place and in any case I was a bit of a tomboy who didn't have time to mess about with things like hair. Anyway when I got the summons I was very frightened.

Trembling, I knocked on the study door and entered when told to. Miss Bradley was sitting at her desk. She barely looked at me and said in a gruff voice "We have been given a blazer by one of the older girls because it is now too small for her. I think it may fit you."

She stood up and held the blazer so I could try it on. It fitted beautifully. I was then handed a letter and told "Here is the girl's address. Please write to her to thank her. You may go now."

Stuttering a "Thank you very much", I left.

The allowance for my free uniform hadn't included a blazer and I had longed desperately to have one. This was heaven. I had a lovely smart blazer with the beautiful lamb embroidered on the pocket. I couldn't wish for more and I treasured it for the rest of my schooldays and wore it till it became very shabby and threadbare, and my arms stuck out from the too small sleeves, but it was almost worth the humiliation I'd suffered on the platform that day.

Although I was a scholarship girl who had most things free, school dinners, milk, uniform and books, I was never ever made to feel inferior in this respect. Indeed some of the girls were quite envious in one way. At this time schoolbooks were scarce and every year we had to sell our old ones to be passed on to the form below. Neat names at the front were crossed out and the new ones entered. They were priced according to their age and wear.

Every year I got absolutely new books and when I came to sell them I was allowed to keep the money. This was a great treat for me and my mother. The other girls used to exclaim about how lucky I was because they had to buy other books out of the money they got and most of them were old and dog-eared. Unfortunately I had six brothers who seemed to delight in scribbling all over them and ripping out blank pages to make paper aeroplanes so, although my books were new, quite a few of them were 'priced down.'

My problem was not having the money to keep up with the other girls. It was pure vanity on my part because no one else thought anything about it.

At the Christmas party one year I had to go in school uniform whilst the others wore pretty dresses. I didn't mind this too much. What embarrassed me was when we went into the room where the party was being held, we were each given a piece of paper with the title of a song on it. We were supposed to sing this until we found others with the same song. It was very funny really. All the tinny soprano voices belting out popular songs. Unfortunately for me we didn't have a radio at home at that time and I had never heard my song before. It was 'I DON'T WANT TO SET THE WORLD ON FIRE.'

In the middle of all this 'melodious' noise, I walked around shouting the title. I pretty soon learned the tune when I matched up with the others and it is still included in my repertoire of 'songs to sing in the bath.'

DAD

There was absolutely no doubt that our Dad was a very creative under-estimated man. He also frightened us to death, for he could be very fierce and would give a loud roar when he was annoyed. But I don't remember him ever hitting any of us and he could be surprisingly kind at times.

Figure 7 Mam and Dad, Alice and Albert Bond,

He was always carving things out of wood, such as a wonderful Red Indian Chief with full headdress, beautifully painted. Once he decorated a plant pot, painting it yellow and blue and making it look like a windmill. This was put on the window ledge bringing a little bit of colour to our drab back yard. It looked very pretty but unfortunately George and I had a bit of a fight, which resulted in our knocking the pot off the windowsill and breaking it. We were terrified and wondered what dire punishment awaited us.

Dad calmly sat us both down and looking very sad said, "You know I put an awful lot of work into making that windmill. I am very disappointed in you both. I thought you would have been more careful about something you knew your mother and I were proud of."

No shouting, no temper. I don't know how George felt but I was thoroughly ashamed of myself, more than I would have been if I had been given a good telling off.

He made a magnificent Spanish Galleon, fashioning tiny cannons that poked through holes in the hull, and larger cannons resting on gun carriages that were on the deck. He waxed string, which he formed into tiny ladders connecting one deck to another. It was a wonderful piece of work but I don't know what happened to it; perhaps it was sold.

Figure 8 Dad, Albert Bond, in his Dad's allotment.

Before Dad was called up in the navy, Fairfield School held a Drama Festival and we were all asked to submit a play to be considered for the production. One play was to be chosen from each form, acted, and then judged at special showings. The preliminary judges couldn't decide which of two plays should be chosen from our form and, as a concession decided both were worthy. One play, a very colourful fairy-tale, had magnificent costumes and scenery and the other 'A Lesson for Delia', needed no wardrobe or scenery, just one essential prop.

Dad and I wrote a 'Lesson for Delia', although to be honest it was mostly Dad's work, an astonishing achievement by a man with very little formal education.

The beautiful fairy-tale production got a well-deserved first prize and our play, well... We had two mishaps, which didn't help our chances. We had two leading ladies, one of whom got an infectious illness just before dress rehearsal, so I had to take over at the last minute. This obviously didn't help our chances, but the second reason proved to be our downfall despite being quite funny. Our second leading lady had polio when young and had been in an iron lung for a long time. As part of her therapy afterwards she took voice production lessons and had a beautiful speaking voice, which alone should have won us a prize.

The essential prop for our play was a bag of caramels. Sweets being rationed at the time, this was a real treat. We were very lucky (or not, as the case may be) because one of our cast had an uncle who knew someone who knew someone else who provided us with a box full of caramels. These were guarded jealously, and we were very good and, although sorely tempted, didn't try them even for the dress rehearsal.

Scene two came and we dived into the caramels with relish, chewing enthusiastically. Unfortunately, they must have been black-market sweets and had an action something like glue. Our teeth were stuck firmly together making it rather difficult to enunciate our words clearly. The audience didn't know how to react so, of course, they reckoned it was a farce and laughed accordingly. It was meant to be a serious look at the lives of schoolgirls, but I doubt anyone realised this. The poor leading lady who was so proud of her voice was mortified. Naturally the judges were as mystified as the rest of the audience, so it was perfectly understandable why we didn't get a prize.

This didn't unduly put out Dad; he thought it extremely funny and was quite proud that his contribution had been chosen anyway.

As I said before, Dad was desperate to join the navy and after putting himself in a job that, unlike the railways, wasn't reserved, was soon called up. After a period of training at Pompeii (Portsmouth) he was assigned to HMS Jamaica and travelled to quite a few places, but mostly the ship was based at Scapa Flow to escort the Russian convoys. His time on the 'Jamaica' appeared to have been quite enjoyable, if you can call service in wartime enjoyable.

Figure 9 HMS Jamaica

He was hospitalised when he got a carbuncle, the site of which was kept secret from us youngsters. Of course, because of the secrecy, we realised it must have been on his bum or on some other part which children in those days loved to snigger about. It appears to have been a very large, painful swelling and by the time he was released from hospital - he had been sent to Baguley hospital, which was reserved for servicemen and women at the time - he missed his ship.

Quite some time later, when I had completely forgotten this conversation, I received a phone call from a 'Sir' somebody or other, who told me one version of what had happened. The Captain of the 'Loyalty' had been taken ill after D-Day and this gentleman was installed as Acting Captain for what was supposed to be just a routine clearing-up operation in the English Channel.

The ex-captain said he had been one of the sailors trapped in the bathroom and he had a horrendous time trying to break his way out. He escaped, suffering almost terminal burns and injuries, and was in hospital for two years. Although he was new to the ship and didn't know many of the personnel, because Dad was by far the oldest sailor he recognised him when he went on deck. Dad was indeed on the deck and something certainly fell on him. The Captain then said, however, that the heavy object had fallen onto his legs, thereby trapping him.

Rita's dolls' house, the money hard won for the shop, and our Dad, all went down with the ship.

My mind, however, was put at ease on one score by the Captain. For years I had imagined Dad stuck in the engine room shovelling tons of coal and sleeping on an uncomfortable hammock with dozens of other sailors. Not so, said the gentleman. HMS 'Loyalty' was an Algerine type vessel, a very modern ship. It was oil or diesel fired and Dad, being an Acting Leading Stoker, would have his own cabin. He asked if he was a trained engineer and when I replied that he had no formal training, he was astonished.

"Your father must have been a very clever man to rise to that rank. The running of the engine room in that class of ship required a great deal of skill and I admire him immensely, I know it would have been beyond me to master all those controls and gauges."

TEA LEAVES DOWN THE TOILET

I had nothing, literally nothing, except my school uniform to wear. This is a lament heard from women through the ages but in my case, it was absolutely true. I had my school uniform and the square necked summer dresses. They had small flowers in the colours of our schoolhouses; pink for rose, yellow for daffodil, green for shamrock, and my colour, blue for the Scottish thistle. They were quite pretty but still school uniform, and Elsie went to the same school and would be sure to have a nice dress for the occasion.

I kept mithering Mam for a new frock but to no avail; she had no money. Tired of my moaning she asked her younger sister, my Auntie Lil, if she could help – she was a machinist but instead of the hoped-for dress run up from a remnant, Auntie Lil gave Mam one of her frocks.

It was 8 years and 2 sizes wrong for me but being desperate I thought "in for a penny in for a pound", gathered the skirt up around the belt and put our George's socks in Marjorie Birtwell's bra so I could fill out some of the front.

Marjorie was a year older than me and passed all her clothes on. Lately the only things she'd grown out of seemed to be her bras – the last things I wanted or needed at that stage.

The dress was quite pretty, pale green with small flowers. I didn't feel quite so bad when I put it on but on reflection must have looked a real fright.

So with a dab of phul-nana powder, borrowed out of Mam's handbag, on my nose and o-do-ro-no under my arms (all the girls at school wore this but I didn't really need it, I just used it because everyone else did), I set off with my friend Elsie to our first dance at the local church hall, two 13 year olds excited and feeling quite grown-up.

We got cups of tea and rock cakes and sat on a bench swinging our legs and listening to the music. Then I suddenly noticed a dreadful smell. I moved along the bench, and it followed me. So, it wasn't Elsie, it was me. It was a pungent unpleasant aroma, which I had often smelt on grown-ups. Oh, Oh, I thought, I know what this is...

Just then a pimply youth in army cadet uniform asked me to dance. Mindful of the noxious smell coming from me but not wanting to spoil my first chance of a dance with a boy, I allowed him to escort me onto the floor.

Luckily for me his dance lessons hadn't extended as far as 'how to hold your partner' so he was quite happy to follow my lead which consisted of my sticking my whole body out away from him, just touching his shoulder with one hand and stretching our arms out to their full extent with the other.

We shuffled awkwardly along the floor, his thick army boots clanging in time to his whispered "One, two" and then a louder "Together" as he determinedly clicked his heels.

This very uncomfortable position, along with the heat and the ever-stronger smell, caused the lad to say "Hot in here, shall we go outside?"

My reaction to this was immediate and grateful, so with relief we walked into the fresh air. We then had the sort of highly unintellectual and embarrassing conversation that young teenagers often indulge in.

"Nice Dance?"

"Yes".

"Did you get a rock cake?"

"I did".
"It was really like a rock wasn't it, ha ha?"

"Yes".

Then "Can I have a kiss?"

Reluctantly I agreed, again adopting the position of keeping my armpits as far away from his nose as I could. Our lips met, tightly closed together and teeth collided in a fierce way; it wasn't very pleasant. My first kiss, I certainly wasn't impressed. We parted, he because he said he had an early training session with the cadets, and me because I felt utterly wretched and upset. I went into the hall and signalled to a plainly relieved-looking Elsie I was going home.

Crying all the way home I rushed into Mam's worried arms and told her that I had 'started' and I didn't like it. "If that is what being grown-up is all about then I not going to put up with it."

Previously I had been told that "Something will happen to you soon and when it does tell me and I'll tell you what to do".

I believe they have now started to come back into 'fashion' especially in hotels that have a lot of people in transit from holidays abroad. That's why I always give hotel
rooms a quick inspection before I go to bed!!!

Before we were married, our family thought Leo my other half, was posh; well he did live in a house with a bath, hot water and inside toilet.

He must also have led a very sheltered life because when he went on holiday with a friend and his mother, he had never seen or even heard of 'Bugs'. Leo was about 14 at the time and he stayed at the B & B in Blackpool one night before his friend arrived. Next morning, he was covered in raised red lumps but wasn't bothered because he thought he had a heat rash.

The next night he was lying in bed talking with his friend, when they saw a creature walking along the bed. Straight away his friend shouted 'a bug, that's a bug' and called out for his mother who took her son off to stay in her room while Leo slept downstairs on the sofa.

The owner of the B & B denied any knowledge of the creatures but the two lads knew what they had seen.

They all went home the next day and when Leo told his mother what had happened she panicked, pushed Leo and his case into the garden, emptied the case on the grass and made Leo take off all his clothes; a good job it was spring and not too cold. After inspecting him she sent him upstairs for a bath while she rifled through the contents of the case looking for any stray intruders.

Apparently there weren't any but that was my OH's first sight of the pesky little creatures.

HE WANTS HIS CAKE AND HIS HA'PENNY AS WELL

I don't often look at the 'Hatches, Matches and Dispatches' column in the local newspaper, but this time a name at the top caught my eye:

> BOND 'Billy'. Suddenly at home, William Bond (52), very dearly loved father of ... grandfather of ... and brother of...

Naturally I looked closer. Could it be? The age fitted; he would have been about two in 1943. The number of siblings was about right. I wondered if this could be Uncle Charlie's boy; one of my cousins whose name I didn't know, whom I had never seen. Suddenly it all came back to me, the scandal, and sniggering, whispered conversations.

Uncle Charlie's first wife Auntie Marie was a slim, dainty and very elegant young woman. She looked rather like a pretty version of Wallis Simpson and according to Grandma she dressed like her and spent like her too.

We later learned that Auntie Marie had consumption. It was a very virulent form and she was taken into Stepping Hill, Hospital, Stockport, for an operation where they collapsed one of her lungs. Although she went to a Derbyshire convalescent home for a time, it was no use and she died round about 1940 or 41.

Uncle Charlie sold up their home in Hazel Grove and taking one or two bits of furniture with him, moved into Gran and Granddad's cottage flat in Openshaw.

Gran kept saying she was rather worried about 'our Charlie'. "He never goes out. It's either work or overtime with him. He comes home exhausted and just falls asleep in the chair. He should get out more!"

Grandma became quite sick towards the end of the war. She had what they called a 'split' heart. I thought it was probably caused through her crying such a lot. She started to make visits to our house, which followed the same pattern. A knock on the front door and Grandma sobbing uncontrollably into a wet hankie held to her face.

I knew straight away that something awful had happened because Mam didn't come forward with a cup of tea, which she always put into a visitor's hand as soon as they stepped into the room.

We had one of those black, old fashioned fireplaces in our kitchen with an oven at the side which usually had some sort of stew brewing in it, and a side plate which held a kettle forever boiling, ready to refresh the teapot, which was kept warm at the side of the oven to be renewed when the tea became too stewed.

Very under-rated and useful, these ovens were always welcoming, giving out mouth-watering smells, and with oven shelves, which, wrapped in old coats, warmed our beds in the winter. Mam hated it though because she was the one who had to black-lead it every week. Once or twice I was given the job but it was so dirty and messy and you had to fiddle to get into all the fancy bits so that your hands and nails became ingrained with the black lead. I soon gave it up and left it to my poor Mam to finish.

Anyway, after the whispering and sympathetic clucking noises from the lobby had been interrupted a few times by us kids, the pair retired to the outside lavvy. Not the most salubrious of places, but the only private place around.

Outside lavatories in slum terraced houses were usually dry (apart from minor accidents on the floor) and that's probably the best thing anyone can say about them. Whitewashed, occasionally, we kids loved to pick off the flaky bits and dig into the bubbles with our nails, making more flaky bits. The floor always had a dandruffy coating, which lined the parts of the stone floor free of newspapers.

Granddad Tom, Grandma's husband, was meticulous about his lavatory paper. He measured newspaper, collected from neighbours, into regulation-sized squares, in which he bored holes to thread string through. These squares were then hung neatly on the lavvy door. When he had stockpiled a lot of these bundles he would send us a supply and for a short time our lav. would be tidy. Tidy, but frustrating because you'd find an interesting bit of a story in the paper, only to discover the most juices pieces had gone, flushed down the basin never to be seen again.

After the whispering in the lobby, which was very irritating because try as I may I couldn't hear a word they said, Mam poured out two cups of tea on the way out to the back. The pair then retired to the lav after first putting a plank over the seat so they could sit; not comfortably, but consolingly close on top of their makeshift seat. Ear-wigging from the backyard all I could hear was sobs and "Oh dear, dear dear me," and "I don't believe it" coming tantalisingly through the thin walls.

Occasionally one of my brothers would wail "Mam, Mam, hurry up. I want to go". "Aw, come on Mam I can't wait." And, getting frustrated with the constant interruptions, Mam answered one of the laments by saying, "Go to Mrs Casson and ask to use her lav". Completely untruthfully she got the reply, "Mr Casson's in there and he'll be ages and ages, he's taken his paper with him. Hurry up Mam, perlease."

"Go on the coal and stop mithering me," was Mam's reply.

It appeared that the same woman had gone to the house, this time with a pram. At one end were new-born twins, the baby Gran had previously seen was at the other end of the pram, and holding on to the handles of the pram was a toddler of about two or three.

Gran said she felt her heart split in two as the woman told her story. The children were Charlie's. She desperately wanted him to go and live with them permanently and give her more money for their keep. Charlie had repeatedly made excuses, the latest one being that his parents needed him to look after them, as they were getting old and frail.

Gran's voice became very unsteady, and so did her posture. "I was perfectly fit and healthy until all this trouble. We'll all be better off without him and I think perhaps you would be too," she muttered.

The woman, Annie, went off, after refusing a drink of tea, leaving Gran to share her shock and horror with Tom.

It was decided that this was the final straw. Charlie's bags were packed and he was unceremoniously kicked out of the house. When Mam told her sisters that Charlie had left with his tail between his legs, Auntie Ann, the feistiest of the sisters, said "And that's where he should have kept it. It would have saved an awful lot of trouble if he had".

Uncle Charlie, a very fastidious man, obviously couldn't stand the noise and squalor of a big family and kept his options open by having a bolthole at Gran's. It was a case, as Gran put it, of "Wanting his cake and his ha'penny as well".

Mam got in touch with the woman "Annie" and tried for a time to help her, for she felt that the poor woman had been treated very badly, but they lost contact after a while. The rest of the family never saw or heard from Charlie and his family again.

After this Gran started to look very old and weary and started to have problems with her heart and stomach. Sadly for her it wasn't the end of the scandals, for one of her other son's, Jim, also brought his problems home.

PEGGY

Rarely had our street seen such a vision as the one I saw when I opened the door; blonde hair and make-up perfect, small hat placed perkily over one eye, beige suit, fox fur flung carelessly across one shoulder, beige high heels. She arrived in a cloud of expensive perfume. "Hello Joan, I'm your Auntie Peggy. Is your mother in?" said the vision.

I gawped, then muttered "Just a minute. I'll get me Mam".

I silently signalled to Mam about the visitor and she whispered back, "Tidy up, I'll keep her talking at the door for a minute."

Dashing inside I grabbed handfuls of toys, clothes and other stuff littered around the room and with difficulty, for it was already full, pushed them into a cupboard. Grabbing armfuls of freshly ironed clothes, I threw them into the parlour and then pulled at Mam's skirt to show her things were reasonable tidy.

Most parlours in those days were very tidy, very musty and used only for funerals, wakes and visitors. Ours was definitely none of those things. It was used as a junk room to house all the rubbish accumulated in a houseful of children. It was certainly not suitable for a visitor, especially a visitor like Auntie Peggy.

Seating herself gingerly on the edge of a wooden kitchen chair – I don't ever remember our house owning anything like an armchair or a sofa – Peggy sipped the tea pushed into her hand while Mam waited to hear what earth shattering news had brought the lady from her home in Hazel Grove to us.

After a few pleasantries, including the latest news on Uncle Jim who had been stationed in Burma for most of the war, Peggy explained. "I heard from friends that Silcock's, the greengrocers at the top of your street, on Cross Street, was getting a supply of oranges today. I thought I'd try for some. I've been unlucky when they've come round our way."

"Oh" said Mam, very surprised. "I believe they <u>are</u> getting some - should be queuing for them very soon. Have you brought Peter's ration book with you? They are only giving them for children under five."

Peggy's face fell. "Well, er. No, I'm afraid I never thought about that."

"Not to worry" said Mam, "I've got three books, so you can have one of mine".

Peggy renewed her lipstick while Mam tidied her hair, put on a finger of lipstick and a dab of Evening in Paris scent behind her ears, obviously trying to keep up with her sister-in-law's delicious smell, then the two set off. Quite a disparate pair they made. Mam was pretty but very homely and certainly had no claim to elegance, whilst Peggy was the height of fashion.

Mam came back later carrying her oranges and in a really black mood. "Cheeky flamer, who does she think she is, strutting down here as if she owned the place, looking down her nose at us. She even had the cheek to give me advice on how to stop having babies! Her of all people. Anyway, she caught the bus on Hyde Road and went back home. And another thing, I'm sure she had already got oranges on Peter's book and only came here so she could scrounge some extra off our books."

I knew why Mam was annoyed about her giving advice on babies. I may have sat quietly in the corner when Mam's sisters came once a month, but I hardly missed a word they said. Peggy was an acknowledged beauty, could get any man she wanted. It appeared that the only one she wanted was one of the dirt-track riders at Belle Vue. He was married, she got pregnant, and things looked bleak for the lady.

Dad's brother Jim, quite a ladies man and very personable, had admired Peggy from afar, never dreaming she would look his way. She looked, went out with him, confessed her problem and Jim and she got married, thereby saving her honour and giving Jim the woman he had always wanted. They rented a sunshine semi in Hazel Grove and a few years later Peter was born. It was an idyllic situation.

"The dirty young madam" was Gran's reply. "It's a good job you didn't tell me afore I had me tea else I wouldn't have fancied it, and it was a lovely bit of ham too. I'd have been sorry to have missed out on it."

Everyone thought Gran's frailty was because of all the traumas she'd been through, so the 'loving couple' decided to take her on holiday with them. They had booked a caravan in Wales and Gran was very excited about her trip. I don't think she had ever been on holiday before.

After she came back from her holiday, we had the usual visit from Gran. Tears in the lobby, this time mixed with indignation, a trip to the outside lavvy with a comforting cuppa, and whispered comments we tried in vain to hear.

It appeared the caravan was very old and very rickety. Gran deposited her small suitcase on the double bed that was at one end, only to be told by Millie that "Oh no love, me and Jim are sleeping there. We'll make you up a bed at the other end of the van.

The table and small sofa were converted to a bed, which was to be Gran's home for the next week.

"I've never been so frightened or embarrassed in my life", said Gran. "Every night and morning too, the noise and shaking from that there end of the caravan had to be heard to be believed. I was sure the blessed van was going to turn right over. What with that and the seagulls having a barn dance on the roof every morning, I swear I never got a wink of sleep."

"To make matters worse they had to dismantle my bed every morning so's we could eat. I took to sleeping on the sofa during the day and never went out all week. I left it to them to go gadding about on their own. You'd think he would have had more respect for his mother. Once or twice wouldn't have been so bad, but it was going on all the time. I was too ashamed to say anything to them but honestly Alice, I'm so tired I could sleep for a week."

I'm ashamed to say that the four sisters were in hysterics when they heard the story. I thought they'd have had more sympathy for poor Gran but the only sympathy they had was for Auntie Lil. "Flipping good job you didn't hitch up with him our Lil. Arthur knew what he was talking about when he told Alice not to let you get involved with him."

It wasn't long before Millie and Jim found a house and they moved in, taking Peter along when they got married after the divorce came through. Unhappily, Gran's health got steadily worse and her trip to our house with the tale about her holiday was to be the last outing she made. It wasn't necessarily the problems with her sons that had made her ill, but Gran had developed a bad heart and stomach cancer and lingered for a long while getting thin and frail. Mam had for a long time gone down to their house once a week to make sure they were all right, but now she started to go two or three times a week, to clean and try to make meals to tempt Gran. Sadly for quite a long time before she died, the poor lady existed only on the Sanatogen wine, Lucozade and Complan, which my Mam fed to her.

It came out that Annie was a well-known prostitute. Poor Uncle John had probably never seen a prostitute before and he probably thought his friends were interfering when they tried to warn him. What proved the last straw for the poor man was the fact that not only was Annie a prostitute, but she was also using her teenage daughter as well and the two of them would bring 'clients' home when John was working. They lazed about all the time, sleeping or getting made-up to go out, and neglected John and the other children.

The papers at the time told the story 'suicide and murder whilst of unsound mind'. Just a bald statement. Poor Uncle John, what could he do? Being a very honourable man, he couldn't turn the family out, and how could he leave his poor little girl with the dreadful woman he had married? If he had confided in the sisters they would have sorted things out pretty sharpish. George's mother, the despised moneylender, became a tower of strength, helping to console the family and saying she would have taken John and the baby in herself if she'd realized what was going on. Auntie Lil's husband was all set to sort Annie out after the funeral and had to be physically restrained. But as they said "That woman isn't worth getting into trouble for. Nothing we say can have the slightest effect on her and won't bring John and the baby back."

John, such a shy naive man, would have been too shamed to talk to his sisters, and wouldn't have liked his sisters to know such women existed.

Annie was a Roman Catholic, and such is human nature that the sisters tarred all RC's with the same brush. Mam finally accepted that I was marrying into the church but one of her sisters was so biased that she refused to come to my wedding. Two or three years later, however, what went round came round when her own daughter had to get married...to a Catholic.

Figure 14 Me and Granddad Tom on my wedding day.

THE ACCOMPLICE

We were all terrified of Mr Cooper, the old man who lived across from us at the back. He'd bark and shout and grizzle whenever he saw us. And you'd never believe the fuss he made when a ball banged against his lavvy door. Cursing and swearing – he used words we'd never heard before.

The first time the ball hit his back gate was an accident, but his response was so very interesting that it proved an irresistible target.

It took two or three direct hits before a red face peered out preceding a body fighting braces. "Clear off" he roared, waving a furious paper. "Damn kids! You near gave me a heart attack. You'll break the blasted door down one of these days, and then just – you – watch – out."

By this time, we had made our escape, giggling nervously in one of the other backyards, jostling for a peep through an enlarged knothole in the gate.

Mr Cooper had also waged a lifelong battle against the 'demon drink'. He was never short of words to say on this subject. "Devil's brew, that's what it is, devil's brew. I've seen enough of it to last me a lifetime I have. Woe betide any of mine I catch drinking that poison. I'll turf 'em out, bag and baggage."

In contrast to her ramrod-straight husband, Mrs Cooper was waist high and made of gentler metal, her bottom half supported only by the fiercely tight grip she put on her stick. The whitest, tightest, curliest frizz of hair I've ever seen haloed her pale face. Neatly dressed, usually in black, she softened her neck with lighter coloured scarves fastened by magnificent brooches.

Their house by our standards was very posh, contrasting tidily with our shambles. The table always wore a chenille cloth centred with a bowl of fruit which I coveted with the envy of someone to whom a piece of fruit was a Christmas treat and oranges were reserved for the very youngest children.

"What? But... But Mam, I wrote that for a test at school ages and ages ago when I was evacuated. How on earth did it get to the Co-op Bakery?"

"Well, as your Dad said, it seemed that his boss was one of the judges at a competition run by the Co-op. The judges all decided to disqualify you but he'd felt guilty about voting against you and he'd kept the paper. He used to see you when you went to collect Dad's wages in your school uniform on a Friday, connected the name, and realised it was you who'd written the piece. He knew Dad had eight children and felt even guiltier then, so he gave it to Dad as a keepsake."

Curiouser and curiouser. "What competition?" I queried. "I didn't know about any competition. And what's wrong with it anyhow? It looks all right to me."

Off-handedly Mam replied, "Oh it was a sort of handwriting competition run by the Co-op and you were in line for the first prize. But just trust you, ya daft ha'porth. You put you wanted to be a reporter on the Daily EXPRESS. If you'd put the Herald or even the Dispatch you'd have won."

As we hardly ever had enough money in our house for essentials like food, luxuries such as newspapers were only seen wrapped round fish and chips, I knew that the little ten year old had plucked the name from out of the air; from a hoarding, someone else's house; maybe even from a cut-up square in the lavvy.

I couldn't see any justice in this decision and felt very angry. Even if I had been a posh kid, if I'd won a prize then that should have been that. And thinking of the prize that might have been, I went very quiet.

Although he showed no outward sign of being pleased, Dad must have been secretly very proud that I was going to a High school. He insisted I went every Friday to collect his wages. This I hated doing, partly because it was a chore having to lug a heavy schoolbag off the bus and down the street leading to the bakery, and secondly, because the bakery was near to the Gas Works on Grey Mare Lane, Beswick. The smell, particularly when the wind was in the wrong direction, which it always seemed to be on a Friday, was absolutely awful; it made me gag. But I didn't stand a chance, for my Mother was also very keen to get Dad's wages a day early. Opinion was stacked against me and I had to go.

The job that Dad had gone for when he needed his suit in a hurry had been as a stoker at the Co-op bakery in Beswick. He applied for this hard and dirty job firstly because it was a lot more money than he got on the railways and also because it wasn't a safe occupation. Dad desperately wanted to be called up, as his lifelong ambition had been to join the navy. Gran had stopped him joining when he was young and then he got married and had a family, and he thought if he was called up then no one could accuse him of shirking his responsibility.

Dad, quite rightly as it turned out, believed his mother resented him because she let his other brothers do anything they wanted. "Why she even let Jim have a motor bike", he once said.

When Gran was very ill and my mother was the only one of the daughters-in-law who cared for or even visited her, Gran confided her secret. She told my mother how much she appreciated what a good daughter-in-law she was and explained why she had resented Arthur. "I was five months pregnant when I got married. My family considered I was snooty and called me 'Our Lady Mary'. You can understand that I was faced with a mixture of shame and smugness from my relatives, particularly my brothers. I bitterly resented having to get married and because of that I very wrongly resented Arthur.

Who knows what would have happened if Dad had joined the navy when he was a young man. Probably none of us would ever have been born!!!

Book 2: MOVING ON (To a Photo Finish)

Figure 15 Joan L Riley

This continues my journey from 'The Age of Innocence' a wartime memoir as I 'Moved On' to a much more contented and moderately successful life, looking for work, taking on second jobs until I got married and eventually in 1960 I started working for a TV Company. This was a time when Granada TV was only a few years old and I watched it change from being just one of the regional companies to become one of the most popular and respected of all the companies.

Sometimes people behind the scenes can see a different picture from the one on the screen. I worked in some very interesting departments one of the first was as a copy taker in the News Room and I was only the third person to hear about President Kennedy's assassination and Granada was the first company in Britain to break the story.

Some of the stories are funny, some homely and some tragic, witness when I typed a transcript of the Moors Murder tape.

I worked for Granada for almost thirty years finishing up as a Picture Editor. Some of the stories in these books illustrate just how naïve I and many others of my generation were, and some of us still are.

ROUND PEG

Dad was determined I should be a teacher. I'd given him hope when I passed my scholarship and he believed that from then on it was only a matter of time before his ambition was realised. Unfortunately, events conspired against him.

My mother and I kept miathering him to let me leave school early and at first he was adamant. However, being away in the navy weakened his resolve and finally he found the pressure too much and gave in.

Mam wanted me to leave because she welcomed the idea of an extra wage coming in and also because she didn't have the same ambition for me as dad. I was not unhappy at school but felt I couldn't keep up with the other girls as far as pocket money, clothes and treats were concerned and I considered once I had a job I would be able to afford any luxury I wanted. How little I knew. With hindsight I could have stayed on at school and do what I later did when working, that is get an extra job in the evenings and weekends. I was, too naïve to realise this and desperately wanted to leave.

Mam decided that I should have a trade and wanted me to join my Auntie Lil as a machinist. This was too much for dad who dug his heels in and absolutely refused to allow it. "I'm not having my girl working in a sweat shop. Think of something more suitable or I'll withdraw my consent," he said.

Mr and Mrs Storey ran the cake shop on Gorton Lane. It was a fine business and Mam had a little job there, cleaning. Once a month on Saturday night, the Storey's arranged that there would be some 'fancy cakes' left over which they gave to my mother, knowing she 'entertained her three sister's to afternoon tea' on every third Sunday in the month: the sisters taking it in turns.

My six brothers knew very well when the delicious 'fancies' were around and my poor mother had to devise ways of hiding the cakes from Saturday night until Sunday afternoon. They would be secreted in various places; inside a piano stool, inside or under pans in the kitchen or, and this was the favourite place, underneath a pile of pots ready to be washed up – it being absolutely unheard of for my brothers to ever wash anything even, at times, themselves but that's another story.

The Storeys knew me because I sometimes visited Mam when she was working and when Mam confided her problem to them they came up with a solution.

The couple had recently bought a large house in Delph near Oldham, which they intended to turn into a kennels cum stud and they told Mam that they would like me to go and work for them as a kennel maid. They had no children of their own and were quite willing to take me under their wing, teach me everything they and their assistant knew, and pay for training should I wish to go further.

Mam was delighted with the idea and, quite rightly thought it would be a good chance for me to get a further education in a good profession. I had no feelings on the matter, either one way or the other. My only experience with animals had been odd encounters with Darkie, the Casson's dog; our George's hens, and various tame mice, which brother John kept until they escaped and mated with the field mice, which then over ran our house. So I had no idea whether I would like the job and quite happily made my way to Delph.

The house was a large imposing stone-built and very elegant place. Mrs Storey, who had been a nurse, was overwhelmingly elegant had very good taste, and had made the house very comfortable and welcoming, and to my eyes, being from a place with no hot water, or bath and outside toilet, it was luxury indeed.

The extremely large sitting room with full-length windows overlooked a very large garden at the back. During my look around the house, which Mrs Storey told me I was quite welcome to do, I soon discovered the large attics. To my delight they were full of all sorts of interesting 'cast-offs' from the previous tenants, among them lots of books and toys. This, I thought was marvellous, if I had time off I could hide myself away up there and have a good old read and rummage.

There were two friendly spaniels based in the house and I found it quite easy to prepare their food and take them on sedate walks around the field at the back. The kennels were situated in a yard at the side of the house and at that time the Storeys had only just started to acquire their 'pedigree' animals. They had two golden retrievers and two great Danes. They were very big animals, which I had little to do with during my first weekend at the Storeys.

I had very little to do during this time and just pottered around trying to make myself useful. On the Monday Mrs Storey decided that she would take me to Oldham to buy me some new shoes. These I badly needed for my others were rather shabby, they had been well worn before Marjorie Birtwell gave them to me, and probably the lady was rather ashamed to be seen with me when wearing them. Considering my job it may perhaps have been more sensible to buy me some wellies or a stout pair of shoes but Mrs S had other ideas. The lady had the same sort of taste as I had in shoes and preferred more feminine footwear. As soon as we entered the shop she spotted the perfect pair. Perfect from both her and my viewpoint. Mid blue suede with a medium size wedge heel and a small lace up front. Very smart. I handed over my clothing coupons and Mrs S paid and we left the shop, me wearing the shoes and both of us extremely satisfied with our purchase.

Wanting to show my appreciation, after Mrs Storey left the house to go to the cake shop, I offered to help the housekeeper scrub the kitchen floor. This floor was a very large stone slabbed floor. Not being very experienced in scrubbing such a large area, and wanted to make a good job of it, I'm afraid I made quite a watery mess and took so long that the housekeeper, who was hovering round trying to prepare the evening meal, got tired of waiting to get near the sink and forcibly took the almost empty bucket and brush away from me and proceeded to wipe up the mess, banishing me from the kitchen to clean myself up.

Obviously, I wasn't considered to be a substitute for a cleaner and next day was informed by Betty, the assistant at the kennels that I was to take the four dogs out for their daily walk. I was quite happy about doing this. After all, what was so difficult about taking dogs out on a lead? Even when Betty told me that one of the Labradors was coming into season and I had to make sure that no stray dogs went near her, I wasn't bothered. I had absolutely no idea what 'coming into season' meant (in those days even girls of 14 were incredibly naïve) and although Betty was very strict about the warning and told me about it two or three times, I took little notice.

Trying to control four large dogs, hell bent on running as fast as they could through the fields proved very strenuous and I had great difficulty keeping up with them but I managed it, just, until…out of the corner of my eye I saw a scruffy looking dog following us from a distance, he was joined by two or three others who stalked us, getting nearer and nearer. Then they started barking and the Labrador bitch became quite excited about the attention she was getting. The three other dogs started to pull one way, guided by me, but this lady had other ideas and started to tug us towards the pack. My arms were nearly pulled out of their sockets as the lead dog caught up with us and started sniffing at the bitch. She stopped abruptly and I tumbled and fell with two of the leads wound round my neck. I kicked at the dog, my arms being full at the time and managed to knock him off. The situation seemed hopeless and I began to realise what "coming into season" meant. Help swiftly arrived in the shape of Betty with a sweeping brush, which she brandished round and round her head like a sword, whacking any animal that came into contact. She disentangled two of the leads off me and shouted, "Now you run back to the house with the Danes and I'll follow. Don't worry, I'll keep these damn mongrels away."

It was little wonder that everyone realised I had absolutely no affinity and was actually frightened of dogs and was definitely not cut out for a job as a kennel maid. So, with absolutely no hard feelings on either side, I was duly despatched home with a new pair of shoes and the Coty lipstick in the gold case, which was on the dressing table in my room, which I had dabbed on my lips when dressing up for the evening meal, £1 wages and my bus fare home. Leaving everyone, including me, quite relieved.

JOB HUNTING

After my disastrous effort at being a kennel maid, I started work as a junior in the accounts dept. of Laurence, Scott and Electromotors.

The Labour Exchange, which was in Chapman St, at the far end near to Ashton old Road, gave me three addresses one for B & S Massey, another Ferguson Palin and the third Laurence Scott. It was decided that Laurence Scott was the favourite purely on account of the fact that it was in Louisa Street right opposite Kenchester Avenue where my Gran and Granddad lived.

Openshaw in those days was a hot spot for engineering firms. There were at least eight in a small area of about a mile square, in Openshaw and Gorton. We took a walk down memory lane recently and could only find one that was still standing...

I was certainly not overworked in the department. I put invoices into number order, filed them, learned how to type and went small errands. The other office junior and I had a great time when we were seconded to look for some obscure file in the archive. The archive was a very large, steel, safe-like room situated directly under the stairs. We had to push and pull to open the heavy doors, which we always opened just wide enough to get in. The room was divided in two and each section was lined, floor to ceiling with steel shelves absolutely filled to the brim with files, boxes and papers.

Obviously, we could spend quite a lot of time 'looking' and took full advantage of the fact by practicing jive steps in the centre of the floor. We spent many a happy half hour and were never questioned as to why we had been so long.

From time to time I was asked to run small errands to other firms, sometimes in the area and once or twice to the centre of Manchester. I had to get a trolley bus at the top of Louisa Street to take me into Piccadilly in the centre of Manchester. These were the errands I enjoyed most.

I had to take an important package one day, to a firm in the middle of Piccadilly.

I had to walk through the beautiful gardens to get there and the whole experience was quite uplifting.

When I got back to Laurence Scott, the lady accountant was waiting for me and took me onto one side. "Where on earth have you been, what have you been doing, we've been worried sick about you?"

"Oh", I replied, completely innocently. "I'd never been inside Lewis's before, so I thought I'd go and look and see what sort of things they were selling. It was marvellous, I've never seen to many lovely things before.

The supervisor, a woman who had taken over when the male accountant was called up, started to have a coughing fit. When she had finished, she said, quite calmly. "Don't you know you have been wasting the firm's time by wandering around all over the place. It just isn't good enough, Joan. I want you to promise me it won't happen again."

"Oh I'm very sorry Mrs Lane, but it seemed such a shame to waste the tram fare when I was so near to Lewis's, but I do promise not to waste time again."

The poor lady had another coughing fit, after which she gently pushed me away and told me to go back to my desk, where there was a pile of filing waiting.

Shortly after this, I was moved, or promoted I suppose you could call it, to the switchboard. This was the old plug and cord type, and I absolutely loved the job. Even better was a marvellous machine, the teleprinter, which it was part of my job to operate. Unlike a telex machine, this was permanently connected to the Norwich branch, and I couldn't get over the feeling of wonderment when it starting clattering away with messages coming all the way through from Norwich. I used to worry that my messages wouldn't go through, because it seemed so strange that they were travelling such a long way and so quickly, but they always did.

After about 18 months, a young woman, Marie, who had been in the WRENS came back to work. She had been the switchboard operator before, and her job had been kept open for her. So I was transferred to the typing pool.

The pool was at the other end of the switchboard area, and red-haired Marie and I got on quite well and she told me very exciting stories of her time in the WRENS. I never thought it strange that I lost my job because of her. She had come back rather later than other people who had been in the war. We found out much later that the reason was because she had had an affair with a married officer, got pregnant, and then had the baby, a girl.

Most of the work in the pool was with dictaphones. These were largish machines on a trolley and the wax cylinders, on which the clerks dictated their letters, estimates etc, were put on the machines, and we played them back, whilst listening on headphones. When we'd emptied the cylinders, they were put onto another machine, which shaved the previous messages away, thus making them ready for use again.

Some of the clerks were very good at dictating but others – well, they hummed and aaahed and made so many mistakes that we spent most of our time rubbing out their mistakes. As each document had at least three copies, this was a very messy and time- wasting task.

I got fed up with this and started to type everything in 'rough' first, and then was able to type things straight off without any mistakes. This made things much easier and soon the whole of the pool started to do the same thing. I couldn't understand why we hadn't been told to do this before.

My wages were about £1.0.1p a week, which I gave to my mother who gave me back, spends of, usually five shillings. This didn't go very far and I did something I should have done when I was at school, and then I would have had no need to leave...I got part-time jobs.

The first one was collecting tickets on the Caterpillar ride at Belle Vue, Manchester, during the Easter holidays. This was temporary but gave me a taste for extracurricular activities. Then I started work four days and weekends at Kidds Milk Bar in Cross Street. I worked from 6 till 10 30 on weekdays, 2 till 11 0 on Saturday and 2 till 10 on Sunday for the princely sum of £1` a week. This was quite a decent wage in those days and I thoroughly enjoyed the job. Quite a lot of the customers were teenagers and we all had quite a few laughs. The milk bar was divided into two, the shop and a small area where there were a few tables and chairs and it was a good meeting place for women shopping, people coming out of the cinema and teenagers getting together.

During my almost two years there, I was never offered any refreshments by the Kidds. The only time I got a break was when the Kidds went on holiday, leaving Mr Kidd's brother and wife in charge. This was the very best time I had there. Every evening they would insist I got a tea and biscuit break in their back room and I was told I could help myself to any cold drink or ice cream I wanted. I never did, partly because after two or three weeks of serving cornets and wafers, I was heartily sick of the sight of ice cream and it was to be quite a few years before I fancied it again.

I managed to pay for two holidays out of my earnings, both to Butlins at Filey. One with Elsie and the other with Audrey.

Elsie and I had great expectations about our holiday and were rather worried that it would be too posh and too refined for us. Our only reference to the place were the pre-war posters showing elegant women in flowing dresses and big hats, and men with bryl-creamed hair and natty blazers. Nothing could have been further from the truth. The place was packed with families, plump mums and dads with hankies knotted round their heads, showing off knobbly knees, lots of youngsters and quite a few teenager. Not a single sight of floating dresses or natty blazers. We fitted in quite well.

Elsie and I were determined to get the most of our time there and decided to join in the fancy-dress competition. Elsie was soon suited. She took a sheet off the bed and dressed as an Egyptian handmaiden.

I puzzled and puzzled about what to do, then had an idea. I went to the roller-skating rink and asked the manager if I could borrow a pair of skates for the competition. At first, he was adamant he wouldn't let them out of his sight, then he relented, went in his office and came out with some very smart skating boots. "You must take special care of these" he said, "Now promise me. These are my special winning skates. You must bring them back tomorrow morning without fail." Excitedly I promised.

In the chalet I tied two pillows from our beds round my back and front with belts. The pillows were plastic and brightly coloured, one blue and one pink. Elsie and I wrote on the inside of two box lids the words "MAKING SURE" in bold letters and wedged them on the pillows.

The pair of us set off for the ballroom where the parade was being held, me carrying the skates around my neck. Once inside, I changed into them and then found out to my horror that all the contestants had to parade round the ballroom in a circle. The problem was that I had never worn a pair of skates in my life and couldn't skate for toffee. Elsie helped me on to the ballroom floor, where a rather nice young man took my arm and with Elsie's help escorted my round the floor. The poor lad had a very bad time of it for my arms were going all over the place, my legs twisted round and round each other in an effort to keep my balance. I kept twisting and stumbling and in the end one or two other people helped the boy.

I was completely oblivious to what was going on around me and, if I heard laughter never associated it with my gyrations.

When the winners were announced, I was absolutely and completely astonished to hear that I had won "The Most Comical".

As I was taking my skates off afterwards, people kept coming up to congratulate me. Most of the comments were on the lines of "What a marvellous skater you must be to put on a show like that." And "Best laugh I've had in a long time...wonderful performance." Little did they know it was certainly not put on?

The manager of the rink smiled when I told him I'd won. "Told you they were winning skates, didn't I, he said?

(verbatim) onto a large screen.

This was invaluable as most of the people at the meeting were almost profoundly deaf. It was fascinating: the modern machine is only the quarter of the size of the one I used 60 years ago. It projects onto a small computer screen and then onto a large screen that everyone can see. The keys no longer have symbols on them, although the design is almost the same. The operator told me that when she was a student, they still used the paper roll to type on. She was fantastically quick and typed at the same speed as everyone spoke. I marvelled at how much the system had changed and also at the many uses to which it has been adapted, not only to assist deaf people but also in court reporting, for events and meetings, and for text on the television.

I believe there are now two societies for this procedure: the British Institute of Verbatim reporters

(**BIVR.org.uk**), who work in many spheres of the law such as the High Court, and the

Professional Association of Speech-to-Text Reporters

(**AVSTTR.org.uk**), which is mainly concerned with helping people who are

deaf/blind.

More than 60 years ago I read about a new form of phonetic typewriting, It was called 'The Palantype Tapewriting System' and had just being introduced from America. The machine was less than half the width of a normal typewriter and the keys were different from the QWERTY normal; some of the keys having two symbols on them so you could press several keys at once to form a syllable, a word or a phrase because they were based on sound rather than spelling out each letter

Apparently once mastered you could type much faster than on a normal typewriter and faster than shorthand and being phonetic could be taken down in any language. The transcript came out on a narrow band of paper and could, with just a few lessons, be transcribed by a typist in her own language. Because it could be used for any language it was just starting to be used in the United Nations and even today on old American films you can see operators sitting on a small desk in the courtroom typing on these machines.

I recently accompanied my husband to a talk about cochlea implants

and there was a Palantype typist projecting everything that was said at the meeting

(verbatim) onto a large screen.

This was invaluable as most of the people at the meeting were almost profoundly deaf. It was fascinating: the modern machine is only the quarter of the size of the one I used 60 years ago. It projects onto a small computer screen and then onto a large screen that everyone can see. The keys no longer have symbols on them, although the design is almost the same. The operator told me that when she was a student, they still used the paper roll to type on. She was fantastically quick and typed at the same speed as everyone spoke. I marvelled at how much the system had changed and also at the many uses to which it has been adapted, not only to assist deaf people but also in court reporting, for events and meetings, and for text on the television.

I believe there are now two societies for this procedure: the British Institute of Verbatim reporters

(**BIVR.org.uk)**, who work in many spheres of the law such as the High Court, and the

Professional Association of Speech-to-Text Reporters

(**AVSTTR.org.uk**), which is mainly concerned with helping people who are deaf/blind.

LEND A HAND ON THE LAND

I had worked at Kidd's milk bar/ice cream parlour for about two years until one day Mrs Kidd took me on one side. Now Mrs K rarely spoke to me so this was quite a surprise. "I'm sorry Joan", she said, "We are going to have to let you go. Business isn't very good and we can't afford to keep you any longer." This was a complete shock because I hadn't noticed that business had gone down but I accepted the reason for having to leave. It was a shame because Audrey and I would have to have a re-think about our holiday now as I wouldn't have any money.

A couple of weeks later I was looking in the window of Myers a la Mode dress shop in Cross Street. I was admiring a suit which I knew I couldn't possible afford when I felt a tap on my shoulder. I looked round and saw the Kidds daughter She was perhaps three years older than me and I rarely saw her because she was usually at work or out with her boy friend, but she had always been very friendly.

We chatted for a few minutes and then started to walk down the street together.

Out of the blue she suddenly said, "I had a row with my mother about her asking you to leave I never agreed with her".

"Oh that was all right," I answered, "If business was going down there was nothing else they could do."

"Oh so that's what she told you, is it? It's even worse that she didn't give you a chance to defend yourself."

I started to get worried. Had they suspected me of taking some money or something?

"Why. What on earth am I supposed to have done?"

"Well, it seems my mother started to get jealous and thought there was something going on with you and my dad. I told her and told her that it was her imagination but you know what she's like when she gets a bee in her bonnet. There's no reasoning with her. She said you joked and whispered together and he would put his arms around you. "I was utterly flabbergasted. "What do you mean, carrying on with...of all people, your dad." "Well, that's what she thought. She told him to get rid of you but he was adamant he wouldn't and said she was talking rubbish. Because he stuck up for you she thought he really was sweet on you and that made things worse."

"Honestly Dorothy, I really don't know how your mother could think such a thing. I used to laugh and joke with your dad, but I laugh and joke with everyone. He sometime put his arms round my shoulder, but I thought he was being fatherly, although I didn't like it very much and tried to dodge out of the way. Goodness me, he's even older than my father would have been if he were alive. He's an old man."

It was very nice that Dorothy stuck up for me, but I was very annoyed that Mrs Kidd had thought such a thing, especially as I'd worked there for such a long time.

Audrey and I had been to Butlins the year before but now had to have a re-think about our holidays. Audrey found a cutting in the paper, which asked "Volunteers wanted to 'Lend a Hand on the Land' during holidays. Pay for your own transport to the site and nominal payment for board and lodging."

We sent for details and realised we could just about afford the fare and board. We would be paid for our work so this would give us our "spends". We chose farms just outside Newquay, at a place called Tregurrion near Newquay or a place that sounded something like that. The rail journey was quite long, but we were very excited and the time just flew by. There were one or two other people waiting at the station as we waited together for our transport to take us to the camp. We all scrambled on the farm truck when it came for us and were taken to what had been a prisoner of war camp.

The camp was still staffed by Germen ex-prisoners of war who were waiting either to be repatriated or to get permission to stay in England. They did the cooking and cleaning and were given priority for any farm work when it came along. We were expected to do chores every day but nothing too hard.

On the first night, the Germans had organised a dance so that we could all get to know each other. There was tea and sandwiches and cake laid on and the music was from an old gramophone worked by two of the ex-prisoners. It was a very jolly evening and the three of us, for we had immediately become friends with a London girl who was the same age as we were and was on her own. We though Margaret was very glamorous and sophisticated because she worked at Elstree studios. In fact, she was very ordinary and was the office girl but this didn't take away the excitement of the fact that she was part of the "film" world.

We danced with each other and with the young Germans. Towards the end of the dance one of the older men got me up to dance. He told me his name was Heinz and he was the chief cook. Although he was very pleasant and interesting to talk to, his dancing was very strange indeed. He held me clamped very tightly to his side as he propelled me round the room. To be fair, it <u>was </u>in time to the music, but was a sort of cross between a goose-step and a fox trot. One arm was held tight across my waist, the other completely outstretched. He used this arm as a pump to help him steer across the room. Very strange routine indeed. Being very interested in anything unusual, I asked him about his work in the kitchens. He told me they were very clean and well equipped. There was a cool room where meat and sausages were hung. He was waiting to be repatriated home to his wife and children and he showed me a photograph, which I duly admired. Because of my interest he asked me if I would like to see his room and the kitchen and mentioned that German sausages were interesting, they were bigger than the English kind.

Eager to learn, I went with him to his room. The prisoners had their own quarters, which were mostly shared, but being in charge, he had a room of his own. He locked his door. "Why have you locked the door," I said. "Oh, there's always someone hanging around and I didn't want them to come into the room." I wasn't particularly worried about this but thought it strange when we had only come to collect the kitchen keys.

I sat on the bed as he rummaged in his cupboard. He sat down next to me and kissed me. It was completely unexpected and was, I know now, a French kiss, which I had never had before, my romantic encounter being the teeth-banging kiss when I was thirteen and one or two chaste kisses from casual boyfriends.

"Why have you kissed me like that?" I naively asked.

He looked at me for a long time and then "Oh you are only a baby."

Affronted I replied "I'm 17."

"You are still only a baby," he said. "Come on I'll show you round the kitchens."

It was an interesting tour and the kitchens were indeed well equipped and clean and I had never seen so much food in the fridges and hung around the cold room.

He escorted me back to my dormitory where he kissed my hand and bade me a friendly "Goodnight."

We volunteers were housed in two large barracks with bunk beds lining the walls. Males in one of the buildings, and females in the other. I had a top bunk. The women in our room were mostly older than us and had come with boyfriends or husbands who were in the other dormitory.

One of the older women, who seemed quietly concerned, asked me if I was all right. "We were all wondering where you've been because you came back so much later than everyone else?" "Oh" I said quite innocently. "I've been to Heinz's room and he showed me round the kitchens. Did you know that German sausages are huge? Much bigger than English ones."

There was a stunned, shocked silence, which didn't register with me at the time. My two friends took what I said at its face value, they being just as naïve as me.

My reputation was not improved when I got undressed for bed. You'll understand what I mean when I say that I had spent two years in needlework class making a baby's nightgown. Every week, the teacher would undo my herringbone stitching on the hem, (I never could get the hang of that stitch), and tell me to do it again until one day she took the garment off me, and holding it gingerly between her fingers said. "I'll get rid of this. It is dirty and disgusting and I can tell right you now that you'll never make a seamstress."

When I explain this you will understand why my hand-made pyjamas had been brought only for use in an emergency.

The offending pyjamas were badly made, the sleeves didn't match, the buttons didn't fit the buttonholes and one side was longer than the other. But I wasn't very worried because I had read in a magazine that southern people were very sophisticated and didn't wear anything in bed.

There was no light on but little did I realise that I was illuminated by moonlight when I stripped off naked to climb into the top bunk, well when I heard a few gasps of disgust I resolved to ask my London friend if Londoners went to bed naked or just some of them. Margaret had never heard of the practice so from then on, I wore the same as at home, my knickers and bra.

Heinz turned out to be a real friend. He asked three of the youngest Germans to take us under their wing and show us around the countryside. They were as good as their word and we had a lovely time, walking through the lanes and riding on, borrowed, bikes. My particular friend was also called Heinz. He was only about 19 and had been in the Luftwaffe. He wanted to be a doctor and was trying to study as he waited to be sent home.

One day we climbed a steep cliff and, exhausted, we collapsed at the top and started talking about what we wanted to do with our lives. Heinz told us about his ambition to be a doctor and from his "expert" knowledge that Margaret would have a difficult childbirth. We thought this was rubbish because Margaret had what you could call "child-bearing" hips.

"I" he said "would find it easy having babies". This again sounded ridiculous for I was very slim and boyish. "If Hitler had seen you he would have made you a German mother" he told me.

What, that stupid looking man with the funny moustache. Not blooming likely I thought. Heinz went on to explain that in order to keep the Aryan race pure, German officers were instructed to marry fair-haired girls of proven pure blood and make them the mothers of Aryan children. I supposedly fitted the bill of a pure Aryan. I didn't know whether to be flattered or very, very annoyed. I just didn't say anything, just grunted.

On the Monday morning we were collected by a dirty old farm van and told we would be picking potatoes. Oh good we thought, we'll get some spends. We were taken to a very big field where a tractor had been busy churning up the ground to reveal row upon row of potatoes, which we collected in sacks. It was very tiring work and before long our arms and knees were sore. Then to make matters worse, it started to rain, heavily. The field became a mud bath.

We three girls had not come prepared for farm work. Heaven knows what we thought farm work would be. The best we could do was summer frocks and sandals, certainly no use in a muddy field.

It was decided at lunchtime that the weather was too bad to continue so, after a meal of sandwiches and water, we were taken back to camp. I can't say any of us were very sorry. It was back breaking work. That was the end of our "Lend a Hand". There was little work to be had and the Germans and experienced helpers had first preference, so we had very little money to do anything and were grateful for our German companions.

Audrey and I had learned a little German at school and when we played table tennis one night, started to count our score in the scant German we had, and I also asked some of the boys if they had a Bleistift (a pencil). The shocked look on the faces of the German boys was hysterical. They thought we could speak the language and were worried about whether we had understood what they were saying about us. We had quite a bit of fun teasing them about what they had said, although we didn't have a clue.

The other women in our room soon began to realise that we were just rather silly, naïve girls and that I wasn't the 'floosie' they thought I was. They even accepted the fact that I roamed round the camp and cycled in my shorts. Shorts in those days were quite longish and baggy. Mine, which had been borrowed, were very tight, very short white pique. I thought I looked like one of the American college girls in films. Obviously, the women had a different opinion. However, apart from calling me the 'girl in the very short shorts', I seemed to have been accepted.

We were all very pleased when we received an invitation to a dance at the local RAF camp on the following Saturday. We were very excited, and I again wore the white suit, with a peplum, which made me look older and which poor Heinze had misread, thinking I was a 'woman of the world'.

A large RAF truck came to pick us up and we were helped into it by some of the non-commissioned officers who had organised the dance.

The very large barracks had been beautifully decorated. There were even two colourful 'strobe' lights, which twinkled and cast shadows around the floor. There was a proper band and a magnificent buffet laid out.

We had never seen such food before, all the food we had was rationed and very basic, nothing fancy at all. Here there were chicken and mushroom vol-au-vents, sausages on sticks, dainty triangle sandwiches with the crusts taken off, and lovely cakes. The catering staff had really done us proud and we certainly did the spread justice.

There was a shortage of single girls so the three of us were very popular. We couldn't get round the floor before someone would tap our partner on the shoulder and excuse him. This was very thirsty work so we made use of the drinks on offer. All non-alcoholic, or so we thought. I tasted a drink, which I thought delicious. I was told it was cider, or apple juice. I don't know how much I drank, but it must a have been quite a lot.

We had a marvellous time and were quite sorry when we had to leave. The truck pulled up outside the room and we all went outside. Once outside I started to feel rather dizzy and my legs felt like jelly. I don't remember anything after that.

The next morning, I woke up nice and early and found myself, fully dressed, lying on one of the empty bottom bunks.

"Do you know" I said, "I don't remember coming back last night."

"Oh don't you" said one of the older women. "I'm certainly not surprised you were blind drunk and I'm surprised you haven't got a hangover this morning."

"Of course, I haven't a hangover, I didn't drink anything, only apple juice. So I can't have been drunk"

"You silly girl," she said. "Don't you know you were drinking Scrumpy, a local cider which is very, very strong? Just how much did you have?"

"Oh lots of it. At least ten glasses, I was very thirsty."

The women all snorted. "All we can say is you are very lucky not to be sick this morning. I don't know, you girls, you keep getting yourselves into all sorts of trouble. Just be careful in future."

We had a lovely cheap holiday and were sorry when it came to an end. Audrey and I wrote to Margaret and she replied for a while but, as is usual with holiday friendships, this petered out and I never found out if she had a bad childbirth. Coincidentally the young airman was right about me. After my son was born, the young doctor who delivered him told me I had good pelvic measurements. Sadly, we never heard from or about the Germans and that was a shame because they were very nice people.

THE LIGHT

I walked into the Jig and Tool Drawing office, a naïve 18 year old with a tray of Earl Haigh Poppies slung around my neck.

Some of my friends had told me about the 'lovely fella' who had just started work at the engineering company where I was a typist. "He's just right for you, you'd make a smashing couple" they all said. I dismissed them. My self-esteem was low and I imagined that a spotty callow youth would be the person they had in mind for me.

Quite unprepared I glanced towards the end of the office and casually noticed a tall figure just getting up from a seat. I didn't see his face because as he moved towards me a sharp beam of light shone like a searchlight between us, linking us together. I've never seen anything like it before or since. Rooted to the spot I was unable to move or speak until the clang of my collecting tin dropping to the floor brought me to my senses.

The young man picked the tin up and handed it back to me. I noticed then that he was very attractive, dark haired and with a nice smile. He put money in the tin and held out his hand for a poppy. Grunting unintelligibly I gestured for him to help himself.

I don't remember if I sold poppies to anyone else in that office, I just remember staggering out feeling an utter fool and convinced that everyone, young man included, must think I was mentally defective.

Leo, too, for that was his name as I later found out, had been told of a girl who was 'just right for you'. He didn't see the light, but he must have recognised something about me because as I tottered out he told the girls in the office "that was Joan Bond the girl you told me about".

Although we often met at works functions and dances, where he would dance with me, he didn't ask me out for ages considering, (as he told me years later) that he had only just finished his national service with the RAF, he was too young to settle down knowing it would be serious if we did go out. Eventually he did ask me out and within two weeks asked me to marry him. Now, emotional conflicts, personality difference and the traumas which are inevitable in any marriage, long resolved, we are more contented and probably just as happy as we were when we got married in 1952.

During the time I was waiting for him to change his mind about taking me out, I had begun to think he wasn't interested, so I decided to take up Marjorie's offer of going in a foursome with Bill and Phil two of her friends whilst she would arrange a foursome with Leo and his friend Ted.

I must admit that we had some very good times with the Bill and Phil on their motorbikes even if I almost got us killed on one occasion.

I had a new coat; red, mid-calf length with a fitted waist and fastened at the neck with a matching tie with fur bobbles on the end. It was very smart, and typical "New Look" fashion but highly unsuitable for going on a motorbike. To complete the look, I wore high heels which together made quite a deadly combination.

The two boys looked at me rather strangely, but I thought it was probably admiration. In those days very few people wore crash helmets, so I positioned myself on the pillion pulling my coat up and holding it with one hand whilst hanging on to Phil with the other. We set off towards Glossop and on the way the two boys, as was their usual macho practice set off to race each other. It was very silly but undoubtedly exhilarating and I let go of my coat to get a firmer grip on Phil's back. Straight away my coat got tangled up in the wheels and the bike went spinning out of control. Showing superb control, Phil braked and although I was tossed off the bike, with my coat still tangled I wasn't hurt, and neither was Phil. Luckily the coat – apart from oil on the bottom, which was soon removed, and a very small tear which didn't show– was all right too. It was an extremely lucky escape and but for Phil being such a good driver, there could have been a nasty accident.

This wasn't the only time that Bill and Phil were in competition with each other and this time again I was fortunate to escape Scot-free.

The Social Club secretary at Laurence Scott's, Mr Mason, came to rather a nice arrangement with the Social Club at Ferguson Palin, another engineering firm in Openshaw. F.P. owned Mottram Hall, in Mottram St Andrew near Prestbury, Cheshire. This was a large mansion house set in acres of lovely grounds and was used as a conference centre but also staff were allowed to go there for holidays. It was agreed that Laurence Scott staff could use the Hall for a holiday weekend and Marjorie, Bill and Phil were among the people to sign up for it. I was asked but because I was due to work at the Alhambra Palais dance hall on the Saturday night, I turned down the offer.

It was suggested that I go by train to Wilmslow station on Sunday morning when Phil would pick me up on his bike and I could spend the day with them, coming back with them on the bike.

I had already been to the Hall when I was 13, when my friend Audrey Wilkinson, whose mother worked at Ferguson Palin arranged for the two of us to go on a special week, which had been given to employers for a holiday for their older children. We were very excited, I more than Audrey for I had only ever been on one other holiday – two weeks in a cottage in Red Wharf Bay with my mother and three brothers when I was about five.

Audrey's mother had managed to get some rather nice soft mid grey material which she had made into two pinafore dresses, each trimmed with red on the breast pockets and round the neck and sleeves. Audrey lent one of them to me and very smart we felt, dressed like sisters.

The holiday was even better than I expected. We were in one of the dormitories with some other girls and joined in all the activities; open days where we played the usual games such as egg and spoon, three legged, and sack races etc. The food was lovely and at night we played games or learned to dance with music from an old wind-up gramophone.

One day we decided to go into nearby Prestbury, I suppose we caught the local bus but I'm not quite sure how we got there but anyway we found ourselves in a little village but there didn't seem much to see so we joined a group of people who were standing outside a shop. We asked what they were waiting for, thinking it was a queue for something or other and were quite surprised to find that they were waiting to see Gracie Fields who was visiting a friend in the village. People were holding autograph books and pieces of paper and we managed to get hold of a page from one of the books, which Gracie courteously signed for us. She was a very kind lady and I don't think we realised how fortunate we were to have been at the right place at the right time. Audrey let me keep the scrap of paper and eventually with being shown around to people, it became torn at the creases and I lost it.

Anyway, to get back to the weekend that the other three had at Mottram Hall, I decided to join them on the Sunday and waited outside the railway station in Wilmslow where I was expecting Phil to pick me up. I was surprised to see Bill turn up and he explained that Phil was having trouble with his bike and he had come instead. The ride to the Hall was very pleasant and leisurely, there being no one to race against and we drew up outside the entrance where Marjorie and Phil were waiting. Phil was covered in oil and

I got off the pillion and turned towards Marjorie, Phil stepped forward and very concerned told me that I had a large oil stain on the back of my skirt. I was wearing a fairly new costume, mid grey with a small white pinstripe, fitted jacket and pencil skirt just below the knee. It was a classical style and wouldn't be out of place today.

He asked Marjorie to lend me a dress and he would try to clean the oil off. I started to warm towards him because he seemed so upset and caring (not enough to fancy him because I still fancied Leo) but rather touched by his attitude. He cleaned the skirt perfectly and it had dried out in plenty of time before we set off back home on the bikes.

It must have been nearly a year later, after I had been going out with Leo for some time that Marjorie told me what had really happened.

Apparently, Phil's bike wouldn't start and he accused Bill of doing something to the plugs so that he wouldn't be able to pick me up. As time went on and the bike wouldn't start, Phil agreed to let Bill pick me up but...before he did he had smeared oil on the pillion seat to get his own back not realising that I would be the one to suffer. Perhaps he thought I might notice the oil before I got on the bike but anyway when he saw the damage he had caused he felt very sorry and did his best to make my skirt as good as new. Notwithstanding this little mishap we all had a good time because it was a beautiful summers day and the Hall was just as good as it had been 6 years before.

Incidentally Mottram Hall is now one of the prestigious Spa hotels owned by the De Vere Group.

EXTRA-CURRICULAR ACTIVITIES

After my stint in the ice cream parlour and Belle Vue I got a taste for doing extra work, or rather for the extra money.

Variously I worked in dance halls in the cloakroom, selling clothes from catalogues in Jay's furniture shop, Saturday job at Lewis's, cinema usherette, making ice-lollies in the summer off-season at Hugon's suet factory, and on the door at the Ritz ballroom in Manchester. All very enjoyable.

The dance hall job in the cloakroom suited me very well because I could take it or leave it whenever something better (or better paid) came along and I worked there for quite a few years until the summer when I got married.

The Alhambra Palais, which had formerly been Chick Hibbert's dance hall and was still called this by the locals, was in Openshaw, next door to the Alhambra cinema. Sometimes I worked in the men's' cloakroom, sometimes in the ladies and very occasionally in the tea bar on the balcony.

Among the regulars was Richard, the doorman, small slim, early forties and very wise. He would dispense good advice frequently and although we didn't always agree with him, we were fascinated to hear his point of view. This was in a time of "saving yourself till you got married," a lifestyle most of us mistakenly believed was followed by nearly everyone. One of his 'wise' bits of advice…"You have to practice before you get married. Otherwise you may find out too late that he has a back door key and you a Yale lock."

This advice we (or most of us) were too scared of 'any consequences' to take notice of, relying on finding out if we were compatible until after the wedding.

Another young woman, Audrey worked in the cloakroom with me and her mother looked after the tea bar. Audrey was engaged to a soldier and very proud of the fact. She was collecting things for her bottom drawer and she sometimes showed me things she had bought. I know that clothing was still rationed but reasoned it would have cost the same number of coupons to buy cami-knickers or French knickers instead of the large bloomers, with elastic round the legs, which Audrey, on the advice of her mother, preferred.

Audrey was a larger version of her mother but without the wifely skills. This didn't bother her because her mum was going to live with them or rather, they were going to live with mum, when they got married.

Audrey and the three bridesmaids, I was one of them, (2nd left on the bottom of the picture) all wore pre-war borrowed frocks which were very pretty. It was a lovely wedding. We all saw Audrey's fiancé for the first time and a very nice good-looking young man he was too.

Figure 17 Audrey's Wedding

After the wedding Audrey took time off from the cloakroom and for a short time Betty came to work in the cloakroom with me. Betty had been to Fairfield High School at the same time and although we knew each other, had never been friends before.

Betty, a natural blonde with a good figure, and nice clothes, somehow never seemed to look as glamorous as she wanted. There was always something missing. She was absolutely desperate for a boyfriend and got a crush on one of the regulars at the dance hall. A tall, good-looking boy, he had not the slightest interest in Betty. But

Betty was very persistent until in the end one night he walked her home.

I got both sides of the story from Betty and the boy, Bill, and the versions always matched. He took her home; they had sex against her backyard door and then he walked off. This happened whenever he felt in the mood and Betty was always ready to oblige though she admitted she never enjoyed it.

There was always the danger that she could get pregnant because he was very careless and didn't care if he ejaculated over her coat and skirt. She 'lurved' him quite madly and didn't care, no doubt mistakenly thinking if she did get pregnant, he might just marry her. I told her she had no chance and would be left literally holding the baby, but nothing put her off. When his interest started to wane, she started buying him little presents...a watch, a wallet and she even paid for his shoes to be mended.

One Saturday night Betty, in an attempt to glam herself up, came to work in a red suit with a matching little pillbox hat. The colour really suited her blonde looks, but the overall effect was missing something. She was very excited when she told me Bill was taking her somewhere different that night.

The next day it was the Sunday club at the Palais and as this was limited to members and was very popular, it was certain that Bill would be there.

Betty said she definitely didn't want to be in the men's cloakroom. This was unusual because she would do anything to see 'her Bill' then I realised she had been crying, crying for quite a long time because her face was blotchy, and her eyes swollen. "Whatever's the matter," I asked. Didn't Bill take you home last night."

"Yes, he certainly did she wailed and I am never, never, never going to see or speak to him again."

This was serious; I never thought I'd hear Betty say such a thing. "Good gracious, whatever happened"?

"Well, Bill told me he fancied a walk down the canal path. I was really pleased about that because I was a bit fed up with our back entry. We walked and walked down the

Towpath, then he stopped and said, 'I fancy seeing you with no clothes on tonight, take everything off.' Well, as it was a warm night and I wanted to please him, I took everything off and folded my clothes neatly at the side of the path.

Then he suddenly started coughing and walked off, without even saying goodnight. I thought he'd come back, so I waited, but he didn't.

He was disgusting, leaving me there, naked, at half past eleven at night. I was really frightened and don't know how I managed to get my clothes on and find my way home."

What could I say, Betty was always shocking me but this really was too much to take in. I told her she had had a lucky escape and was right to never want to see him again. It was dreadful and dangerous to leave her alone late at night on the canal path. Heaven only knew what sort of people were lurking there at that time.

Later that evening Bill came into the gent's cloakroom where I gave him the biggest telling off I think he'd ever had. "You always treat Betty dreadfully but this time you've gone far too far. Didn't you realise how much danger you put the poor girl in. I can't tell you how disgusted I am." To his credit he did look very embarrassed and quite upset.

"I know Joan, I did go too far but honestly I couldn't get rid of the girl and thought this would do the trick. I didn't intend to leave her but when I saw her standing there stark naked with her moustaches waving in the breeze and that stupid little red hat on, well I just started to laugh and wanted to get away as far as I could."

"Well," I said, "You've got your wish, she never wants to see you again and neither do I"

Betty was true to her word, she was cured. But her kind nature still pushed her to do daft things. Some days she would bring refreshments down from the balcony café for the band during the interval. She liked to do this because the lads in the band were young and full of fun. They teased her dreadfully, but she took it all in good part.

Betty trying to keep up with fashion wore falsies, squashy plastic inserts worn inside your bra to give you assets you never thought you had, which she imagined gave her the hourglass figure all the fashion magazine were showing as part of the 'new look 'and, as was her nature, she didn't keep this a secret but was quite happy to show the lads what they looked like. Often the lads would say, "Lend us your falsies Bet" and then the band would borrow them to play football round the rehearsal room with Betty good-heartedly joining in the fun.

When Audrey came back to the dance hall after her 'honeymoon period' and after her husband went back from his leave, Betty was quite ready to leave. Neither she nor Bill had made any secret of what had happened, and I think even she began to get fed up with the teasing. I never saw or heard from her again, which was a pity; she was a lovely warm-hearted girl who hadn't deserved to be treated so shabbily.

Various people ran the Palais during my time there. I remember two bank managers whom we thought very rich. We didn't see much of them, they were mostly in the office doing the accounts; and then a middle-aged man who had a pet shop in Ashton old Road took over. He sometimes brought his 11year old daughter with him. She was a very precocious little madam and regaled us with lurid stories about various animals' sex lives.

There was also a hands-on manager who ran the place, arranging special evenings and competitions. One of these 'specials' was organised by Bob Dale who later became quite famous when he presented national sequence dance competitions on television. He was very tall, dark and handsome, always immaculately dressed. He organised a competition with a team of dancers from Holland. It always amazed me that the girls could even stand up in the many-layered dresses, covered in sequins and spangles, but they certainly did and very colourful and pretty they look as they were guided round the floor.

Later there was a blonde manager. He was married with children, but he seemed to attract all the girls, although I could never fathom out why. He left to take up an under-manager's job at the Ritz in Manchester.

Marjorie Peacock and I were very good friends at this time. She fancied Bill who worked in the estimating department at Laurence Scott and would go out on his motorbike with another lad, Phil, who worked in the Tool room. Marjorie persuaded me to go on foursomes with the two lads and in return, if the occasion arose, she would make up a foursome with Leo and Ted. Leo also worked at Laurence Scott and Ted was his friend. I fancied Leo!

Bill and Phil, trying to get in our good books, asked us to go to the Ritz and also invited my mother. We didn't dance, just sat on the balcony and had a couple of drinks as we watched the couples on the floor.

The former manager at the Palais, came over to us and introduced himself to my mother. He then asked Marjorie and I if we would like to work at the Ritz part time in evenings and weekends, Marjorie in the cloakroom and I on the door as a sort of hostess. I was more than willing to do this because these girls wore a very cute uniform. It sort of mixed and matched a white skirt with a red blouse and red trousers with a white blouse.

I had fondly imagined that these outfits were laundered every day and was rather disgusted when I was issued with a pair of red trousers stiff with dried blood. I complained most strongly and was told "Oh don't worry about that. Jess wore them when she had a miscarriage"!

Because I was' young, fresh meat', I got an awful lot of attention on the door, especially from the Jewish boys. One night one of the older men became very persistent and to put him off I told him I had a boyfriend of whom I was very fond. "Just my luck", he said. "I always seem to fancy something in a shop when its closed."

I took all this attention with a pinch of salt and was just very cool and polite. However, one night he pressed a pound note into my hand. Now this was a very large amount of money in those days, almost a weeks' wages. I refused quite strongly but he persisted and said he wanted to treat me because he thought I was such a nice girl. I took it and made sure I always disappeared whenever he appeared.

One night I was surrounded by a group of six or seven boys. They were flirting outrageously, but I tried to ignore them. The under-manager called me over. I thought he was going to tell me off for talking to the lads, even though I was desperately trying to ignore them. "Are those lads inviting you to a party tonight," he said. I replied that they were. "Well for heaven's sake don't even think of going. The party will be you."

I had amused my mother about some of the goings on at the Ritz but when I told her about the money and the party she, unusually for her, put her foot down. "You've got to leave there, at once", She said.

Marjorie had had the same thought and told me she was going to leave whether I did or not. She, too, had had quite enough of the seedier side of Manchester.

It was certainly an education working there. Marjorie learned all about the prostitutes who frequented that area. To get in and out of the cloakroom, people had to go through a turnstile, which needed a coin. To save money, for some of the ladies of the night were very active, they would jump over the gate showing the fact that they had gone into the cloakroom to leave their knickers in their coat pockets. This didn't seem to bother them although poor Marjorie used to get very embarrassed especially when they started to talk about their 'clients'.

I had amused my mother about some of the goings on at the Ritz but when I told her about the money and the party, she unusually for her, put her foot down. "You've got to leave there, at once". She said.

Marjorie had had the same thought and told me she was going to leave whether I did or not. She, too, had had quite enough of the seedier side of Manchester.

THE NEWS ROOM

The ad in the Manchester Evening News looked very interesting. Vacancy for fast typist to type stories from local reporters. Apply to Granada Television etc. A few days later I received a letter asking me to go to the studios for a typing test. This seemed to go down very well and I was told I'd be contacted later. Then, a letter asking me to go for an interview with a Mr David Plowright. David was still news editor but was in the process of moving to the magazine programme as producer. His new office was in a porta-cabin in the car park I knocked and entered and saw a youngish man, very casually sitting at his desk with his legs on the table in front of him. He gestured for me to sit down. He looked at me and then to my surprise said: "What do you think of four-letter words." Coming from a rather formal office this was the last thing I expected and wasn't sure what to say. Flustered, I squeaked: "Oh I don't mind if they are not addressed personally to me". "Mmm… only the girl who had the job before you objected most strongly."

"No, I don't mind" I replied. Then with a nod of dismissal my interview appeared to be over.

I had no idea whether I had got the job or not but as I was supposed to give two weeks' notice to my other part-time job at Bolchover's (a dress fabric distributors), I waited until almost the end of the two weeks, then rang Personnel at Granada. The lady who answered was very surprised and said: "You are supposed to be starting next Monday at 2 o'clock. Haven't you received our letter? Oh, just a minute, she said then I'm very sorry, it's still in my 'out tray'."

I then had to confess to Mr Jacobs, or Jack Hobbs, as I had mistakenly believed he was called - I must have seemed very rude as I called him Mr Hobbs for most of the 18 months I worked there. Mr Jacobs was in charge of the office staff and a very nice, quiet man he was too. He understood perfectly when I told him about my problem. "Oh that's quite all right, I understood you were going to leave this week because I sent your reference off three weeks ago and there was no reason to believe you wouldn't get the job. Here, I'll show you a copy of what I sent." It was indeed a very nice reference.

I had already realised that the television company was an extremely relaxed place. I was to work in Granada's newsroom taking down 'copy', that is, wearing headphones; I would type out news stories, which were phoned in by freelance reporters (or stringers) from all over the north. At that time Yorkshire, Cumbria and Lancashire as well as parts of North Wales and the Isle of Man were part of the Granada region.

On my second day, as I opened the door to the office, a quite famous (then) man was walking out. He pinned me against the door and said "I'm going to have you against that door." Just how do you reply to that sort of statement, I thought? Not wishing to appear as naïve and ignorant as I undoubtedly was, I answered, in my most sophisticated voice. "Oh that's nice". This reply had the effect of my being labelled, "fast" and for a couple of weeks I was subjected to the most subtle and not so subtle suggestions, most of which I allowed to fall on deaf ears, pretending I had no idea what they were talking about.

Happily, it wasn't long before all the men realised just how naïve I really was and then they started to treat me and Joyce (the girl who had started in the same job on the same day as me) with a great deal of respect.

Granada's newsroom was then on the ground floor looking onto Quay Street and next to the car park lodge. At 8 o'clock each night I would take empty flasks to the café and bring tea and coffee back to the office to keep us refreshed for the night. One night on my way out to get the coffee I heard a great deal of noise and a Commissionaire told me that there were literally hundreds of girls screaming for the Beatles outside the car park. They were pushing so violently that the car park barriers were in danger of collapsing and the men were trying to keep control. I was vaguely interested but didn't really know who these Beatles were at that time. As I was talking to the Commissionaire four young men came through the doors and one of them, I think it was John, said "eh doll can youse tell us where the caff is"? I casually answered, "Yes, I'm going there come with me". So me with two empty flasks and these four young men walked and talked all the way to the café, I to get refills and they to get refreshments. If only I had got their autographs!!!

At first, five or six of us worked in a small office until it was decided we would move firstly into a large office on the 5th floor and then to an open plan area immediately above where the original newsroom had once been. We would be sharing with the local magazine people as well; the office was very large. At one end was the studio, separated from the rest of us by a large glass window so that we could see what was going on and the cameras could 'pan' to show the rest of us working in the background. Next was the area where reporters, researchers, directors etc worked, this area was usually fairly empty as their work often took them away from the office; and right at the bottom was the news area. The cameras were on sort of railway lines so that they could move up and down from the studio through to us. Interviews and musical items were often conducted in our area to make for added interest.

All the clerical staff were in NATKE the (national association of theatrical and kinematic employees). The union decided that as we were regularly in vision we should be paid 'performance fees'. We were highly delighted at the prospect, but the management refused to agree. "All out whenever the red light goes on" we were instructed and dutifully we left the office and watched proceedings from televisions in other departments. This completely defeated the object, which was to give the impression of a busy office in the background so, after many meetings, it was agreed that we would be paid.

Then, the union, in their infinite wisdom decided it wasn't fair for us to be paid more than staff in other departments and asked the management for an all-round rise for everyone in NATKE. This, of course, quite rightly, they absolutely refused to do. After many discussions it was decided that Granada would pay the money to a charity, not to us. We never found out what the charity was and suspected it went into the NATKE funds and understandably we were not very amused.

It was a very exciting time, we never knew just what was going to happen, and usually it was something very interesting or amusing. One day I turned to find a large lioness sitting at the side of me. My colleagues were expecting me to scream but I reasoned that as it was sitting there without a cage it must be either old or toothless. It turned out to be neither; it was young and just like a big friendly dog. Another time I had to regularly fill hot water bottles for a glass cage full of snakes and found out that they are not cold and slimy but quite warm and soft.

On one our exits from the office we watched Alan, a very handsome producer/performer on a television in another office. He was fronting an article on silly joke things including a doorbell shaped like a boob, which played a rude song, whoopee cushions and a black fake piece of chest hair that he demonstrated by putting it inside his opened shirt. After the broadcast we made our way back to the office, which was manned by a temporary secretary from the Bureau who was covering for someone on leave. Obviously, she was one of the few people who hadn't seen the broadcast. Quite a good-looking woman she was very unapproachable looking. Her hair severely tied back in a bun; she sat strait-laced working very hard and ignoring everyone. Alan asked me who she was and I told him "A temp." She's a bit frosty faced, just watch me I'll make her smile." Alan went over to the lady and squatted on her desk while he chatted her up. "I've not seen you before do you like working here? You know you have lovely hair I would love to see it loose." Very flattered the lady smiled, blushed and cast her eyes down modestly. Alan had put the hairy chest inside his flies and the effect it had on the lady had to be seen to be believed.

Screaming hysterically, she shouted "Oh you horrible, horrible man" Grabbing her coat off the rack she ran down the corridor. We could hear her screams for quite a while. Bob, the editor looked up and very calmly said. "Someone ring the Bureau for another temp."

One day a very young, very tiny girl with red hair came to the side of our desk and started to chat. She was Scottish and very friendly, but I was certainly glad to have my headphones on when she started to sing. It was Lulu, who was rehearsing for the local magazine shoot and, I believe one of her debut TV performances. She sang, "Shout" almost directly into my ears and she certainly could shout. It was very, very loud.

One researcher, small, dainty and extremely beautiful, was a fervent believer in women's rights and women's lib. When she spoke it was always a complete surprise for her voice although pleasant and melodious, was also very deep and masculine and strange coming from such a feminine woman, but ideally suited to television presenting. She was soon 'discovered' and appeared regularly on television. One day she was conducting an interview with Desmond Morris, the animal expert who appeared fairly regularly on television at that time. This time he had brought a baby chimp with him. Before the rehearsal Vanya behaved in what we believed to be an uncharacteristically maternal way, cooing and pretty boy-ing just as you would to a baby. She held him up in front of her...and then … he wee'd directly into her face. It couldn't have happened to a 'nicer' person. We all had a good laugh and to be fair she laughed just as loudly as the rest of us.

Vanya Kewley, became a very well regarded documentary filmmaker. Her team was one of the first film crews to bring the BIAFRA disaster to the attention of the world. I often watched her films, and soon realised that Vanya was in fact a very brave women who covered quite significant stories. But always I had the memory of her wet face and hair and the way she laughed at the joke.

On evening, the day before Halloween, there was a feature with the King and Queen of the witches, called Maxine and Alex. Maxine looked just as you'd expect a fairy princess to look very long auburn hair falling in waves down her back, long flowing dress, very beautiful to look at with a porcelain skin. Alex the self-styled king also looked the type. Very dark hair, saturnine features and strong nose. His eyes seemed to look straight through you.

After a rehearsal, which was conducted in the small studio at the end of the office, the pair came down to the news area, sat down and started to chat to the duty editor and me. They told us about how Alderley Edge in Cheshire was, to them, a very mystical special place and on Halloween they had a special gathering. I asked if they danced in the nude, I was nothing if not straightforward. But they talked round the question and didn't answer me. Next I put my foot in it again by saying in a joking manner. "I suppose its all a myth that you can cast spells. You can't really, can you?" Maxine put a controlling hand on Alex's shoulder, and he looked at me, very fiercely indeed. Oh dear, I thought, I've really put my foot in it this time, and I felt rather frightened, although I was only joking and didn't mean to be rude.

After a moment or two he said "I have already put a spell on you." Thoughts of Titania and her crush on the donkey-headed Bottom flashed through my mind. "Whaat is it, whaat spell? I asked. "Never you mind," said Alex. "How will I know what the spell is I asked"? "You'll know. When you get home just look at your right foot." I felt much more relieved when he said this, at least I wasn't going to fall in love with someone stupid.

As usual when I got home, I relaxed with a cup of tea and told Leo, my husband, about all the doings of the evening. I started to tell him about Maxine and Alex and suddenly remembered the spell.

Laughing I said, "Alex said he'd put a spell or a curse on me and to look at..." I stared down at my right foot. It was massively swollen..." my right foot I continued. Just look it's horrible. I hope the swelling goes down". Of course it did and everything was back to normal next morning but he taught me a lesson not to joke about things I knew nothing about.

There were times, though, when we had to type sad, and heart-breaking stories and the very worst happened in 1968. I had just finished typing a story and pulled my headphones off when Sally, who was sitting next to me, gave me a push, which nearly knocked me off my chair. I turned and saw she was sobbing. She flung her headset off and just kept shaking her head and saying, "No, No, I can't do it." She then ran out of the office into the nearby toilet.

Putting her headphones on I asked the reporter what he'd said to upset her. He sounded very subdued and almost in tears himself. "I'm sorry. It's this story. It's the transcript of the Moors Murder tape with Leslie Anne Downey. Do you want to carry on?" I agreed and started to type. The reporters always dictated in a staccato journalese way and this style made everything he dictated to me seem unreal. I can't of course remember exactly what was said but it was something like this.

"Mam, Mam, I want my mam" point   Don't, I want to go home" point. Stop it I want me mam" point par. Honest to God, if I don't get home for eight she'll kill me. Point. Please let me go. point end....

After he finished the reporter told me that he had seen and heard some dreadful things in his life and thought he couldn't be moved by anything   "But", he said, "this is the most disturbing thing I've ever heard and I am sure it will haunt me for the rest of my life. "If you were upset by typing it out, don't ever, ever, listen to the tape" he told me.

In the book 'Granada Television The First Generation' there is a piece by Claude Whatham which reads "One night I shall always remember: Michael Parkinson, who was then a staff journalist/researcher and another reporter, arrived ashen – faced. Over very stiff drinks they attempted to convey the horror of their evening. They had been present as the mother of one of the victims of the 'Moors Murderers' listened to the tapes of her daughter's screams as she was being tortured. She had to identify the voice of her child..."

Over the years I've become very angry with the people who keep saying it was inhumane to keep Hindley in prison for so long and an infringement of her civil liberties. I wonder if **they** ever listened to the tape and wondered about the civil liberties of all those poor children and their parents. In my opinion Hindley lived 36 years too long.

OGDENS

Joyce and I started worked on the same day for Granada's newsroom as copy takers and when they put on an extra late news programme, we took turns working the evening shift. During the evening, we got to do more interesting work than just typing stories from the freelance reporters (or stringers) who rang in from all over the north with news they hoped would be used on the local bulletins. At night we sometimes had to get captions or pics to illustrate an item; ring the police and fire brigades to see if there were any major incidents and get the nightly weather forecast from the Met. One of our duties was to ring the Meteorological Office every night and type out the Weather forecast for the following day. This we then took to the Duty Announcer. The Announcer's job was a lonely one; he or she sat in a tiny booth-like office waiting to read out details of forthcoming programmes, changes to the schedule etc. Sometimes the booth was empty whilst they took a well-earned break to the canteen or went for a chat in the control room. We then left the forecast on the desk.

One announcer, a well upholstered gentleman, very friendly, and jovial, was so relaxed that he would have made Dean Martin look nervous   We would always have a chat and a bit of a laugh and sometimes I took him a cup of tea. One day he told me that I wouldn't be seeing him anymore – he was leaving. I said I was very sorry to hear that and asked if there was anything wrong. "Oh no," he said, "I've got a part in a programme. Can't tell you anything about it 'cos it's hush-hush. Keep your fingers crossed and who knows you may be seeing me *in front* of the television for a change soon."

Some months earlier I had been in the ladies chatting to a young woman while we refreshed our make-up and combed our hair. I didn't know the girl very well but asked if there was anything wrong because she looked quite fed up and I thought she had been crying. It appeared that she was a bookings clerk in the casting department and told me she had put in for a promotion to Casting Director, a very good job. She had to put forward ideas for a new family for Coronation Street and was getting depressed because she just couldn't think of anything. Just casually I mentioned that I had lived in a Coronation Street type house and there was a family nearby where the husband, who was a fat slob of a man who liked his ale, and who came up with the most incredible excuses not to work. His wife was a downtrodden little woman, very hard-working and it was she who kept the family together. The young woman just smiled when I said this but made no comment.

Now it could have been a coincidence, I'm not suggesting anything else but...the young woman got her promotion. There was a new family on the street, very similar to the one I had described and ... the announcer's name just happened to be Bernard Youens, who made his fame and fortune as Stan Ogden....

Figure 18 Bernard Youens (Stan Ogden)

KENNEDY

It started out as a normal quiet Friday night in Granada's newsroom. The evening shift was usually uneventful; often the most we could hope for was a story on the ongoing Icelandic Cod Wars, a film clip of Blaster Bates' blasting his latest chimney, a multiple accident or a fire. The office was completely empty apart from Terry, the editor, and myself. Our two desks were pushed together, Terry sitting at one and I facing him at the other. The free-standing television at the side of our desks, positioned so that we could both see it, had the sound turned down very low with Mike Scott presenting 'Scene at 6.30' in the background.

Terry was idly looking at some early copy, looking for a story suitable for the nightly pun, a tradition, which entailed finding the corniest ending to the evening news. I sat doodling waiting for the copy phones to start ringing. The direct line rang, looking up I saw Terry's face change and heard him say, "OK, I'll ring back to check." Imperiously he whispered "Paper in typewriter", a signal meaning a late, important story was coming through which needed to be taken into the studio to be broadcast live on the air. As he dialled on the internal phone, he gestured with a finger across his throat, and said 'forget it', "Kennedy's been shot".

For the next quarter of an hour everything was surreal. I watched Terry dial on the main phone to confirm the original call hadn't been a hoax, and then relay the news to Barry Heads the producer in the studio. I heard Terry say, "News is just coming through that "President Kennedy has been shot." Apparently Barry's reply had been "You'd better be right this time mate." Then the confirming, "Yes, it is true." Almost immediately I saw Mike Scott on screen pick up his phone his face changing to a look of concern as he repeated word for word what Terry had just said. Then "The President, his wife Jackie and others were riding in a motorcade through Dallas, Texas, when shots rang out, we believe one of his aides has been killed, the President we think is alive.." Then, very shortly afterwards, " John F Kennedy, President of the United States is dead".

Suddenly the quiet calm of the office was broken. People came in from goodness knows where: the canteen, pub, and other studios. It was a hive of activity as everyone set about preparing an obituary programme from scratch and news flashes that were broadcast throughout the night. Normally obituary programmes are already on file but the President was a relatively young man, so there was hardly anything prepared and what little there was happened to be locked in the Archive. Eric Harrison who was producing the tribute programme at 11.0clock had to open the archive door with force.

The rest of the evening passed away in a blur. I was typing out copy from the Press Association, Journalists, Famous People, all wanting to pay tribute to the President. As fast as I typed, a researcher or director whisked it away to sub it down for the programme, which was going out at 11 o'clock that night, Friday 22 November 1963.

All those years ago but it is all as clear to me as on that historical evening when I was the third person in Britain to hear the news. The story had come through on short-wave radio to the Stan, an editor at the Press Association in London, he phoned it through immediately to Terry and then almost straight away Terry relayed it to the studio it was broadcast to the whole region. A memorable evening and a foretaste of the instant way news stories are broadcast today.

As a post-script, a few years ago there was a question asked in the ' Daily Mail answers' column about which company was the first to broadcast news of the assassination. I replied that it was Granada. Then, two rather snide letters saying I was wrong, it was the BBC who did the first broadcast.

Letters from Terry Dobson, and the editor of the Press Association who was on duty that night, were then printed, which confirmed Granada was indeed the first on air with the story. The PA editor saying the other TV Companies were annoyed that Granada had been given the scoop, but it was the only station with the foresight to give out an emergency number in case of such an eventuality. The editor at the Press Association had received the news direct from Dallas on short-wave radio. He relayed exactly what was coming from Dallas straight to Granada newsroom. If you can describe such a tragedy as exciting, then that is exactly what that night was. A point in history, which I for one will never forget.

Granada was the first company in Britain to break the news and all the staff involved felt very honoured to be involved and to receive congratulatory notes from the Granada hierarchy for our work on the night and I got a very nice telex from the PA, thanking me for my contribution.

Years later we went to a neighbour's funeral and at the 'wake' later Phil Griffin, another neighbour who had been a producer at Granada, asked me if I had seen Sir Denis Forman's book in which I was mentioned. Very surprised I told him I hadn't and asked what it was about because Sir Denis didn't know me from Adam. Phil told me that it was about the Kennedy assassination and promised to show me a copy.

When curiosity got the better of me and Phil had obviously forgotten about it, I went to the local library and looked at a copy of the book: 'Persona Granada' by (Sir) Denis Forman. On page three in the preface Sir Denis quoted an account he found in the archives of something I had written, giving the full details of that night in November 1963. He said that it answered an argument that had been going on between Sir Denis, David Plowright and Barrie Heads concerning who had actually be on duty on that historic night and who had given the OK for the item to be broadcast.

Figure 19

To: ~~Tom Filey~~   Date: 29.11.63.

We would like to congratulate you on the way you handled the news of the death of President Kennedy. We were first on television with the news, first to pay tribute, and our late tribute programme was superior to anything seen either on the ITA or BBC. We are very proud of the evening's work.

S.L.B.
C.G.B.
Peers
Forman

GRANADA MCHR
TO GRANADA MANCHESTER
MEMO FROM MCNAE TO HEADS.
I SHARE YOUR PLEASURE AND LOOK FORWARD TO LETTER. PRAISE IS ALWAYS EXHILERATING. AND I TAKE THIS OPPORTUNITY OF PASSING ON THE THANKS OF MY STAFF TO YOUR %SIMPLY MARVELLOUS% COPYTAKER, WHO EASED OUR TASK TREMENDOUSLY.
------ 12.10 25.11.63 WN

GRANADA MCHR

Figure 20 Telex about President Kennedy Shooting

COME UPPANCE

Michael, small, dark and macho, an amalgam of Russian, Jewish, Irish and English ancestry, was one of the sub editors who used to work on evening duty at the television station. In common with others on late shift he would often while away the night by disappearing into the nearest hostelry for a pint, or three, and a chat with the barmaids or any other available lady. But woe betide me if a big story came through and the sub had changed pubs and I couldn't find him!!! Thankfully this rarely happened.

Often the subs would forget the time and rush back at the last possible moment, dictating news scripts fifty to the dozen in an effort to get them ready for the rehearsal deadline and cursing me like mad if I dared to make a mistake. One particular night, not altogether light-heartedly, I dared to remark that Mike was lucky I was such a fast typist "else you'd have to leave the pub at least an hour earlier."

Although my mother looked absolutely beautiful in her coffin, She had a coif over her hair and the fronds of hair I could see looked as though they had come from the back of her head. I fretted dreadfully over what I imagined had happened to her but I realised that the person who was my Mam had gone, leaving just a shell behind. This, in a strange way, gave me a little bit of comfort, for I reasoned that if my Mother wasn't in the coffin then the essential part of her must have gone somewhere else.

It was rather strange to see the street lined with old people, some of them 30 years older than my mother. She had helped all of them with shopping, washing, cleaning windows and putting up curtains. They were all there to see her off in style and yet she had gone before them.

George sold Mam's little terraced house in Gloucester Street; it had been used as surety for his butcher shop in Dukinfield and John and Malcolm moved in with him into the flat above the shop. Eric, Alan and I were married at that time and Jimmy, well he walked away after the funeral and it was some time before the rest of the family heard from him...he was living with friends from the church he attended and Rita, our sister came to live with us. Although about 20 at the time, Rita had learning difficulties and it was felt that it would be too difficult for her to understand what was going on if she went to the funeral, so Leo's mother looked after her.

Quite a while after the funeral we had a bit of a family conference, where it was decided that George, Alan, Eric and my husband Leo would travel to Plymouth in George's van, George, Alan and Leo taking turns driving. Mam and Leo's mother had taken a trip to Plymouth a few years earlier to attend a ceremony to mark the opening of the beautiful memorials on the Hoe. They found it very upsetting to walk round these lovely (I think marble) tributes to the thousands of, mostly young; men killed in the Navy, and associated services, the names of all the men were picked out in gold, giving their rank and were on memorial plates, which had the year, they died at the top.

Mam often spoke about the trip, however, how emotional it was and how it was nice that she had somewhere to go if she wanted to remember Dad on one of his anniversaries, there not being any grave to take flowers to.

Because it was such an important place for our mother it was decided that my brothers and Leo would take her ashes and scatter them in front of Dad's name on the Hoe.

If you can picture the scene…about 4 o'clock in the morning, three of the boys, for they were all in their early twenties, asleep in the back, Leo driving…a police car, sirens blaring passed them and flagged them down.

Leo stopped, wound down his window, and asked the policeman who had come to the van, "Hello sir, can we help you? "Do you know what speed you were driving lad? Said the copper. "Well yes, as a matter of fact I do, I glanced at the speedo. just before you stopped us, 49 miles per hour" "Mmm, well actually it was 47.5."

"Is there a problem then?" asked Leo. This is an open road so I'm entitled to do 50."

"Indeed it is an open road, but you are certainly not entitled to do any more than 30 miles in that van. Weren't you aware of that? Is this your van, sir?" By this time the policeman was probably thinking he'd caught someone with a stolen vehicle. My husband, rather puzzled answered, "No, it's my brother-in-laws".

"Oh, I see, your brother in law's you say? And where might you be going in your 'brother in law's van' he asked rather sarcastically".

"To Plymouth" Leo answered. "And what is our business there, sir". "We are going to scatter my mother in law's ashes on the Hoe."

The policeman was looking even more sceptical at this stage. But at this point George put his head, blonde stubble on his chin and rumpled shirt, through the opening at the back of the van and said "Yes, sir this is my van."

"Oh, and do you know the speed limit on vans? "Yes" said my brother. "30 miles per hour." "Then why, pray did you not tell your brother-in-law"?

"Sorry, sir, it completely skipped my mind what with us all being so upset and everything." "I see, and why are you upset and just what is your business in Devon?"

"Well." said George. "We are going to Plymouth Hoe to sprinkle my mother's ashes in front of my dad's name on the Memorial on the Hoe".

This seemed rather too farfetched to be true and the policeman sniffed and said, "Really, is that so. I must say that's the first time I've heard that one."

Just then another hand was pushed out from the back of the van holding an urn and followed by the head of another one of the brothers, half asleep, with an overnight growth on his face, "Here, sir, this is the urn, would you like to look inside?"

It was difficult whether the constable really had a coughing fit at this time, but in any case, he was spluttering and wiping his eyes as completely defeated he shook his head. "I don't know, that's a new one on me. I'll probably get a few free drinks on the strength of that one. I'll let you off this time, but look on, if you lads put a foot wrong, I'll have you. Now go along with you and good luck."…

PAT

After working in the Newsroom for quite a few years, I decided I wanted to work full time and managed to get a job in the Promotions Dept. This department was responsible for all the 'on-air' publicity for programmes, especially local ones. The promotion scriptwriters compose scripts for the duty announcers and selected clips (or trailers) of varying lengths from programmes and films which the Programme Dept. hoped would whet the viewers' appetite and keep them watching. Originally, they also provided black and white slides, often of scenes from films and plays but usually generic ones of the stars. This material was used to fill in any breaks between programmes, which sometimes under-ran and also to fill in if there was a shortage of commercials for a particular slot.

When Granada changed over from black and white to colour, the photographs they had were mostly black and white so new ones were needed. One of my jobs at this time was to arrange for new photographs to be taken of the Coronation Street actors. We arranged a 'mock-up' stills studio outside the Green Room - where the actors rested between rehearsing - and I would look for anyone who wasn't needed for rehearsal or filming and try to persuade them to have their pics taken. In those days, when the Street was only two episodes a week, the actors had plenty of spare time. Sometimes you'd see them knitting, Thelma Barlow would often be seen cutting out a dress or blouse and tacking it in the rehearsal room and they had a card school, the stars of which were Doris Speed (Annie Walker) and Bill Roache (Ken Barlow). Jean Alexander (Hilda) and Bernard Youens (Stan Ogden) would play scribble, which meant that it was relatively easy to get someone to pose for pictures.

However, one of the times I went into the Green Room to sort this out, Pat Phoenix (Elsie Tanner) swept into the room. Now when she had her full make up on, her hair done and was dressed up, she was a splendid sight and had what is called 'presence'. Everyone always stopped what he or she was doing to look at her.

"Get that TV Times girl out of here" she said imperiously pointing to me; this was said to no one in particular. This comment was prophetic on her part because a few years later I would become involved with TV Times but I was on bona-fide Granada business at this time.

We learned early on that if a 'star' said anything or wanted anything or swore obscenely at you then woe betide you if you answered back or failed to do their bidding. It wasn't unknown for some poor menial to get the blame if a scene went wrong and the actor fluffed their lines. Immediately it would be "It's that girl's fault, she upset me" or words to that effect. Bearing this in mind I left the room abruptly. Pat, however, was very kind-hearted and when she found out that I was only doing my job and wasn't some journalist looking for scandal she took me under her wing and we became quite good friends and I sometimes went out on Personal Appearances" with her.

I also went out to lunch a couple of times with Pat, Tony Booth and Tony Warren (the creator of the Street.) At that time Tony Booth was in his 'humble' phase, having just recovered from the dreadful, life-threatening burns he'd endured and had just re-started his relationship with Pat. He was very interesting and told stories of his out-of-body experiences, which don't seem to have made it in reviews of his book.

Later on, he became very very left wing and had some strange ideas but at this time I really enjoyed his company.

He told us that after his accident he apparently died and found himself floating on the ceiling above his body; he spoke of the conversations he'd heard; the people he saw. When he told the doctors and nurses what he had seen and heard they told him that he couldn't possibly have done so from the angle of his bed even if he'd been conscious.

In another experience he went through a tunnel and came out onto a beautiful beach. He was tanned and young and dressed just in white shorts. He was asked whether he wanted the fit young man in shorts or, and here he was shown his dreadfully disfigured body on the bed. He was just about to think (or say) he couldn't determine how he communicated, that there was no choice, of course he wanted to be the fit young man, when he realised that he was making a decision between living and dying and immediately thought "I don't want to die". Upon which he felt himself go back into his battered body.

Sadly, he and Pat didn't get married until she was on her deathbed. Pat told me that she was afraid if they got married then she would become liable for income support for his many children and partners, so they waited until the last minute.

It was an open secret that Pat had had a face-lift or two but no one ever mentioned it, only exclaiming how good she was looking.

I was occasionally given a lift to work by a neighbour from Highdales Road who was a plastic surgeon at Withington Hospital. Being a curious type I asked him one day if he'd done Pat's face-lift. I know it was very undiplomatic of me, but I can often be impulsive. He answered me by saying that he sometimes did cosmetic surgery privately in order to finance the lifesaving and desperately needed surgery on people who were disfigured or badly burned. He neither admitted it to me nor denied it.

Well, Pat told others and me this story, so I don't think I'm giving away any secrets.

Pat was having a lie-in one Saturday morning when she got a phone call from Gerry (I think that was his name), a reporter on a Sunday newspaper. Gerry was a nice man and would do anything rather than embarrass anyone – a welcome change from some of the other journalists. Pat knew him quite well and liked him.

He stuttered and spluttered on the phone until Pat had to ask him "What on earth is the matter. Come on spit it out." He said his editor had insisted that he asked Pat if she'd had a face-lift and that he was sorry to ask but it was more than his job was worth not to do so." This was about the time that newspapers were doing a "cull" of the Manchester based journalists and they were all worried about their jobs. Pat knew this very well and wanted to help the man.

"Where are you", she asked. "In the pub" he answered. Pat lived in two cottages (or maybe it was three), which had been knocked into one rather nice spacious house. It was down a small lane with a pub at the bottom.

"Come up here. My housekeeper I'll let you in," said Pat. Gerry duly presented himself to Pat's bedroom. As she said, "I'm not the prettiest sight without make-up at the best of times but first thing in the morning, well...my hair was all over the place. my three–tooth crown was at the side of the bed. I was smoking a ciggy and asked him out of the corner of my mouth what it was he wanted to ask me. As she said " I was trying to make myself looks as grotesque as possible"

Stuttering and purple in the face he said, "Miss Phoenix, have you er, er ever had a face-lift?"

She beckoned him to come closer "Just look at this", she said, sticking her face into his and pulling the skin up. If I'd had a lift do you think I'd look like this old wreck wouldn't you expect me to look better than this?" she asked him.

Honour was satisfied. Pat hadn't lied and Gerry had an answer for his editor. It must have satisfied him because the story never appeared and Gerry kept his job, for a time at least.

Figure 21 Pat Phoenix (Elsie Tanner)

GRANDDAD'S FORMULA

No one, not even the pension's board knew Granddad Tom's real age. When he reached what he believed was 65, the pensions authority first of all said he didn't exist because his birth hadn't been registered. At this Tom got very upset saying **he** knew he existed and so did his wife and four sons. Then on obtaining proof of baptism they said he did exist but was only 63. Granddad hotly disputed this saying that his parents had probably had a block christening for himself and two of his brothers; this was quite common in those days to save time and money and that as he was the middle of the boys, he would have been at least two at the time. The pensions people and granddad couldn't agree and granddad swore it was a deliberate plot to cheat him out of his 'rightful' pension.

Although he had a gammy leg, the result of an accident at work, he was a very healthy sprightly man, and lived to the age of either 96 or 98. He was a very keen gardener and kept his garden and allotment immaculate and also cut the lawns and did heavy work for all the widows in the area, both before and after Grandma's death.

When I got engaged to my soon to be husband Leo, his parents were invited to tea by Gran and Granddad. My father-in-law was very taken by Tom's garden especially the beautiful lush green lawns. Although Leo's father had lost an arm in the war and was restricted in what he could do, he, too, loved gardening and asked Tom whether he had any advice to give him on getting a lawn like his. Granddad touched his nose conspiratorially and said, "that's my secret formula", and making no effort to tell him what it was.

Leo's father kept going on at me to find out the secret but told me not to say what I wanted it for. Finally I got Granddad to reveal his secret..."I wee on it" he told me.

Naturally I passed this message on to Leo's dad.

About a month or so later, I was confronted by a very angry Mr Riley (Leo's dad), who asked what Granddad and I were playing at. "Just look at my lawn, it's gone brown and shrivelled up. It wasn't a bad bit of grass before but now, just look at it?"

I confronted Granddad and he asked me what dilution Mr Riley had used. I looked at him blankly. "You put one part urine to 5 or 6 parts water", he said, " why didn't you tell me why you wanted to know about the formula."

After this, the whole family found out what had happened and also discovered that Mr Riley had been going out in the middle of the night, for weeks spraying the lawn. The image of this caused quite some amusement and as he lived in the middle of busy Altrincham Road, we all wondered why he hadn't been arrested. Tom reassured him that if he gave the lawn a good watering it would soon grow back better than ever, which it did.

The postscript to the story only came out years after. My brother George was the Duke of Edinburgh's double when he was younger and like the Duke he began to lose his hair in his early twenties. This upset him very much and he kept asking his brothers to examine his head to see if any hairs were growing on the bald patch. He got increasingly disappointed when they said they couldn't see any.

After a few years he started to wear a hairpiece. This he used to plonk on his head never caring whether or not it was straight or central. The wig resembled a rather mangy red squirrel and was quite hideous. Why red when he was blonde I'll never know? He was completely unselfconscious about it and was quite happy for anyone to re-position it when it was pushed lopsided on his head. It gave us all plenty of laughs and in a way we were secretly disappointed when he, or rather his wife, decided he looked better without it. Years later we learned why he had kept asking about any re-growth...

He confided in my brothers that when he heard about Granddad's formula he reasoned that if it grew grass it could grow hair and he had diligently rubbed wee onto his head every night for months. He gave up when it didn't seem to work. However, after seeing his wig the whole family were in general agreement that he should have persevered a bit more with the 'formula'.

MISTAKEN IDENTITY

Whilst visiting the doctor for a trivial complaint I noticed that his file on me was very large. This was surprising because I seldom, in those days, went to the doctor.

He confirmed my name and then looked enquiringly at me. "How are you coping with your diabetes, Joan?" he said looking rather concerned. My stomach dropped, what did he mean? "Have I got diabetes then?" I asked him. He looked at me quite keenly. "Well, yes, quite a severe case I'm afraid."

I started to get quite panicky as I answered, "I didn't know, nobody ever told me".

He then confirmed my name, "Joan Riley" but when he asked for my address, he suddenly became quite apologetic. "Oh dear, I've been given the wrong file. This is for another Joan Riley." He said moving to the office to get my file. This was much smaller and we both had a bit of a laugh especially when I told him how panicky I was at the thought of a lifetime of needles and injections.

Going forward a few years I happened to sit next to a young woman on the bus and we started to talk about the fact that there must have been a couple of buses taken off because we had waited so long. The woman asked me if I was coming home from work and where I worked. I told her Granada TV. "Oh," she said, "Perhaps you know my friend, Mary Aimsbury, she's worked there a long time." Oh, of course I know Mary," I said " We worked together in the Presentation dept.for quite a few years." We then discussed Mary, her daughter and their horse and Mary's complicated love life and got on very well together. We had quite a few laughs and when I started to get up at my stop I asked her what her name was so that I could tell Mary I'd been talking to her." "Joan Riley" she replied.

"Oh I said, so it's you, is it? The doctor and I got quite confused because of you - my name's Joan Riley, too". I almost missed my stop because we discussed this and had a good laugh about it.

Fast-forward another few years. After I had taken redundancy from Granada, I started to work on the League of Friends tea bar at Wythenshawe Hospital, my husband was Chairman of the League at that time. The tea bar had expanded over the years from a small table with ladies serving tea and biscuits to quite a large concern. It was very well stocked and sold everything from sweets and drinks to sandwiches, toast and hot pies.

The volunteers worked various shift of either two or three hours and the café was opened every day from 10 0 am to 8 0 pm. A few years previously I had changed my shift and when I bumped into two of the volunteers who had previously worked with me, I hadn't seen them for a long time. One of them hugged me quite gently and the other put her hand on my arm. "How are you" she said, very concerned. "Very well, thank you, how are you"? I asked, rather touched that they had seemingly missed me so much. "We've been worried about you and praying for you..." Oh, I thought, they must have missed me more than I realised.

She then continued...."every week at church. We believe you've been very ill indeed the priest has been reading out bulletins on your progress." I realised then what had happened and told them about the mix up at the doctors. Again we had a laugh about it.

A few years later I saw an obituary announcement in the local paper. My namesake had died ...'After a long illness bravely borne.' I felt rather sad about this but thought no more about it until I got a phone call from Edna, a friend I'd worked with at Granada.

"Are you going to the retiree's lunch next month" she asked me. "Well, yes" I replied. "Good" said Edna "I've been driven mad by calls from people saying how sad it was about your death and when was the funeral and was I going and how they hadn't known you'd been ill for such a long time. I told them that as far as I knew you were alive and well, had never ever been ill and it wouldn't have been 'bravely borne' anyway. At least if they see you in person, they'll realise that 'reports of your death have been greatly exaggerated, to quote Mark Twain..."

CAPTAIN'S TREAT

We enjoy cruising and usually ask for a table for 8 to 10 people, thus ensuring that we meet a wide range of interesting people and have nearly always been lucky in this respect.

The Sun Vista, (which sank a few years ago – not I hasten to add when we were on it) was a bit of a rust bucket but we had the cruise of a lifetime it was just one exciting moment after another. The very beautiful Thai and Malaysian girls who served us were the most friendly and courteous people we have ever met – and all for no reward; there was a 'no tipping' policy on board. I often wondered what happened to them when the ship sank. Leo. My husband, being over 6 ft tall was a special favourite with them.

As part of the holiday we spent two days in Singapore and cruised for five days from there through Malaysia and then had a 6-day holiday in Penang.

Most of the people on board the Sun Vista were Australian or Chinese although we were told there were more than 50 nationalities on board. The Aussies were a very refreshing lot extremely laid-back and on the Captain's evening most of them were pushed to find a tie never mind a jacket but no-one seemed to mind. We shared our table with six Australians; all related, most of them ex-pats who had emigrated with their parent's years before. They had all had skin cancer of one sort or another because, as they said, "No-one knew about the sun in those days and we used to stay out in it all day long when we were small." Luckily, they had all been cured but their arms and legs were covered in scars.

One of the ladies and I went to the toilet – the ship being quite old only one cubicle was working and out of it came a very elegant blonde lady. As she was washing her hands I exclaimed, "I notice you are on the Captain's table. (This was directly opposite to ours). It must be very interesting; the Captain seems very charming and handsome." She smiled and said, "I think so too, he's my husband. Collapse of very embarrassed party - me.

My companion had heard the conversation from inside the toilet and when we got back to our table she started to amuse everyone with the story of my faux pas. The gentleman opposite me then started to make funny nodding motions towards the back of my head, I wondered if he had a nervous tic but when I turned round there next to me was the Captain. He bowed and clicked his heels – he was Norwegian, very tall, blonde, very distinguished looking. He said "Sank you Madame for your kind verds. My wife has told me about your conversation." Red-faced I spluttered "Your wife is very lovely", he of course completely agreed with me and then we had a conversation about the ship and what we thought about it and our holiday. He then left.

Later the Australians had ordered wine and were going to sign for it when the waiter said "Oh no, this has already been paid for with the captain's compliments. The captain has said you must order whatever you want." Our wine, which had already been signed for had also been paid.

After dinner we all went to thank the Captain for his kind gesture – now if you've been on a cruise, you'd realise that there are two kinds of people who go on the top table. One lot are poker faced and hardly smile throughout the meal, the others are the life and soul of the party and quite jolly and noisy. The group on this occasion time were mostly Chinese, very serious looking with never a smile. I suspect they were gamblers because the ship had a special casino, which only the very wealthy Chinese were allowed to enter.

The Captain smiled his acknowledgement to us and his wife then said to me "You see it pays to know the right people". I answered quite straight-faced, "Yes, I've never had a pee with a VIP before." At this point the whole table immediately saw the funny side, the inscrutable Chinese people were especially amused and everyone relaxed and had a good laugh. It broke the ice somewhat and possibly the captain thought it was worth paying out for the wine as his companions then had something to smile about.

COINCIDENCE????

One holiday in Menorca we became casual friends of a family; mother who was a nursing sister, father and two children. We sat at adjacent tables in the dining room and exchanged details of places to go and things we'd seen. One evening the family didn't come to dinner. We thought nothing of this, thinking they had come back late from some trip. The next morning the hotel was agog with details of a honeymoon couple, the groom had been killed crossing the road at Mahon; he'd looked the wrong way and the wing mirror of a lorry had caught his head. The young family from the hotel had been near to the accident and the mother had taken care of the poor young man, made him comfortable, gone to the hospital with him and helped the medics there with explanations in English etc. Unfortunately, the boy died and the nurse also helped to comfort his bride.

Arriving home my husband called to see his mother, this was one of the first things he did after a holiday to make sure she was all right. "Oh, Leo" she said, "Mrs Flanagan's son was killed, and I think it was at the same place as you went to, one of those islands." (Mrs Flanagan lived in a house which joined his mothers at the back, and the two ladies were quite good friends, meeting as they did at church) "He was on his honeymoon," Mrs Flanaghan told her. My husband told his mother that it must have been a dreadful coincidence because a young groom had been killed on holiday but he came from Middleton so it couldn't have been Mrs Flanagan's son.

The next morning (a Sunday) Leo's mother phoned after going to church and asked Leo if he would go round to her house? It seemed that Mrs Flanagan had come home with her from church and wanted to speak to him. It actually was Mrs Flanagan's son. His wife came from Middleton and the couple had bought a house there and that was why the report said he was from Middleton.

Mrs Flanagan, who was understandably in a very upset state tearfully told Leo that it was her heartfelt wish to contact the nurse both to thank her and also to find out about her son's last moments. Leo told her he would try to find her, but because we only knew the first names of the family and didn't know where they lived, he didn't hold out much hope. We contacted quite a few travel agents and the hotel itself but with no success.

This all happened in September and the following June we decided to take a holiday, spending the first week at a friend's boarding house in Newquay and the second at a farm in Cheddar. The weather was typically wet and windy, and we didn't go near a beach for the first week. When leaving for Cheddar on the Saturday, the weather was beautiful, the sun was shining and we had put swimsuits on under our shorts, determined to get a few minutes sun-bathing on the way to the farm as the weather looked promising when we left Newquay.

When we saw a sign "To the Beach" we went down narrow lanes and finished up on a long sandy beach. We put our towels down and started to catch the sun, the normal five minutes on each side... After a while it started to get windy, so the pair of us sat up and debated on whether to brave the wind or carry on to Cheddar. We saw a family walking towards us; if we had been lying down we would have missed them because they were walking down by the side of us. It was the family from Menorca. We stood up and screamed at each other and gave one another a customary hug. Leo was then able to tell them he knew the boy's mother. That she was desperate to talk to the nurse and get their address and phone number.

Mrs Flanagan then got her dearest wish, which was to talk to the nurse.

Coincidence or something more? Bear in mind that this was a different time of the year, we were on an isolated beach and if the wind hadn't blown at that split second...who knows. And as the saying goes, "There are more things in heaven and hell than ever you thought of Horatio" or something...?

Another coincidence that happened strangely enough involved another nurse. We had a holiday in Morocco, at Agadir. We were in rather a nice hotel and had a cabin by the side of the swimming pool. One night there was going to be a typical Morocco evening with dancers and entertainment and a couple we had become friendly with came with us to the souk (market) where we bought typical local costumes. Leo had a Kaftan and a turban with matching slippers with curled-up toes whilst I had a very attractive dress (white) lined with gold embroidery and a coat with the same embroidery. It must have looked quite nice because one of the older waiters helped me to adjust the belt and looked at me and said "ah Fatima, Fatima". I discovered later that this wasn't about my weight but a very nice compliment in Arab countries.

We wanted to get a seat near the front so the four of us gave the Head Waiter a rather generous tip to give us a ring-side seat. He winked and promised he would. But, on the night we were quite near the back and asked the waiter why? "Oh", he said quite innocently pointing to the people at the front, "They gave me a better tip", and smiling he walked away. Obviously to an Arab this is just normal bartering. He didn't even offer to give us our tip back.

Anyway, to get back to the coincidence. On our last night we went for a swim and drying myself I reached for my sandals, felt something sharp inside and casually kicked it away. Our cabin was just by the side of the pool and when we went inside I realised that the sharp object was a rather nice necklace that our son Paul had bought me. It was a small blue Wedgewood figure on a silver chain. Something I really treasured because it was a very thoughtful and attractive thing for a young boy to choose.

Our friends at the hotel all came to try and search for it, with no luck. A nurse from Wales who was on a three-week holiday with her mother and young daughter was very sympathetic, telling me that she understood how upset I was, as she would be the same if she had lost something her daughter had bought her. She took our address and telephone number and promised that if anyone found it she could send it back to me.

This was in October and when I got home, I felt very guilty and night after night kept calling myself careless and stupid etc. One night after another night of self-flagellation, I felt a feeling of absolutely beautiful warmth going right through my body and a feeling of peace. It was a very memorable and lovely experience and I didn't thing about the necklace after that.

Then, months later I got a phone call asking if I was the Joan Riley who had been on holiday in Morocco in October. When I replied that I was, the lady on the other end of the phone explained that she was the nurse from Wales and she had got my necklace. Apparently, she had lost our address and had been ringing round all the holiday company in Manchester and the hotel trying to find out our address. It had taken a long time but she had finally been successful.

On the very last day of their three-week holiday a very young Arab boy had gone to them trying to sell them some jewellery. This was quite a common practice and usually people dismiss them, but she asked to look at it and immediately realised that this was my missing necklace. She posted it on to me but refused to tell me how much she had paid for it saying that "it was her present to me". I sent her some beautiful flowers and a great deal of gratitude.

Coincidence, maybe I would have thought it was, except for the beautiful feeling of peace that came over me.

Figure 22 Me and the waiter who took "bribe" with Leo

CAN ANYONE FORETELL THE FUTURE?

The library at the end of Church Lane (now Cambert Lane) was in a very convenient place for me and I used to spend all my spare time there when I was at school. Later when working I still visited and one day looking for something unusual to read, I picked up a book on Palmistry. I studied this quite carefully and practised on the family, reading the different lines on their (sometimes grubby palms).

Then I progressed to one of the girls at work and was disturbed at her reaction when I spoke about a child. I must have hit a nerve somewhere and I gave up this hobby except for trying to read Leo (my husband's) palm after we were married.

Years later for two years running we spent a wonderful holiday at Rock House near Thurleston in Devon. This small family-run holiday was perched on a small cliff at the edge of the sea. I think erosion has swept away quite a lot of the garden now.

The hotel was run by a retired vet from Stockport in Cheshire, his wife, son and his wife, and the vet's elderly mother. It was just like going home and you could practically guarantee that you would soon make friends with all the other guests.

One night, after I had had a couple of lager and limes and was feeling a bit 'merry', Leo, who was also a bit squiffy, told two of the guests that I read palms. Of course the reaction was predictable and the girl persuaded me to read her palm. I was very reluctant but in the end decided it would be easier to do this than to argue any more.

The couple, who were in their mid thirties had a little girl with them. We had a bit of a giggle as I looked at the girl's hand and told her that I could see two strong (probably married) relationships, three children and a small amount of money coming her way very soon if not already. The couple looked at each other but made no comment just making jokes of what I had said.

The next morning, I was inundated with palms, most of the lady guests wanting me to give them a reading. I refused saying that I need two lager and limes and was promised a whole table full that evening if I would promise to do readings. I was a little tired of this game and gave them a definite 'No' I didn't want to do it.

After lunch the vet whispered in my ear that I could go into their kitchen for a cup of tea after the meal – a real treat. But, waiting for me was the vet's mother; hand outstretched with a pleading look in her eyes she asked me to read her palm. I spluttered and said it was only a bit of fun and I couldn't really do it. She insisted and then told me that I had been uncannily accurate when I had done the young woman's reading the night before. Apparently the couple weren't married, the little girl was from the girl's first marriage, she also had a young boy who was with his father (her husband), they were getting a divorce and she was marrying the man she was with when the divorce came through, she was pregnant with her third child and a month previously she had won a couple of hundred pounds on some pools coupon – this had paid for the holiday. I was utterly astonished but to be truthful rather scared as well. I just told the elderly lady a few simple things and vowed never to read palms again.

I almost kept my word but at a party I read a neighbour's hand when I was once again 'merry' and as at Rock House the two marriage line came up. After telling Claire she seemed very interested and kept asking me to tell her more, which I couldn't do. I must admit that it worried me dreadfully when a few years later she split up with her husband and went away with a policeman. Could the fact that I had told her there were two important man in her life have made her discontented with her husband and encouraged her to look for someone else. I decided it was too dangerous to dabble like this and never have since. Well, not palm reading anyway. However, meeting Claire years later she told me not to worry my fortune telling had nothing to do with the split from her husband.

I then decided to try astrology. I got books, ephemeris for various years and diligently looked at the various signs, positions of planets at birth and aspects. It was very compelling reading and with astrology it seem safe to think I had no chance of predicting anything specific, just signs and trends.

Every day on the way home from work at Granada Television I passed a largish building which was the social club headquarters of (I think) the GPO. They held various functions and lectures, and different societies met there on a regular basis. I found out that one of these was an Astrological Society so of course I made enquiries and joined.

Just a small group of people were regulars and we were given guidance on reading and plotting charts by an attractive hippy looking young lady. She would divide us into groups and give us a birthdate to interpret. One week it was Marilyn Monroe's birth date, although we didn't know until after we had done the reading. It was surprisingly accurate showing that she was a Leo and a lot of the characteristics of her sign fitted in with the tragic lady's life.

Next week the 'hippy' lady gave us the birthdates of a newish baby and split us into two groups of four. It was agreed between both groups that this new baby was too OTT to be normal. The aspects were full of music, news, talking and noise. It's ending, and usually you are not supposed to look at anyone's death signs, was very prominent and suggested a suicide probably due to money problems. It was generally agreed that this was an animal or something; it was too unusual to be a person.

We were right it was in fact the newly started Piccadilly (Manchester) Radio Station and although it is still going strong, I suppose it is quite feasible that if it closed down it would be due to money problems.

These small successes persuaded me to enrol for an Astrological Degree course at St John's College which was opposite Granada TV and over the years has been Granada's extra rehearsal space, social club and café and is now a very plush Boutique Hotel. William Roache (Ken Barlow) in Coronation Street also went to one or two of the lectures at the Social Club and although he couldn't guarantee to be free for the evening course at the college because of filming commitments was so interested that he enrolled in a correspondence course and actually got his DF Astrol degree. The course at the college was cancelled due to lack of support so I never took it any further. Bill Roache did do my chart for me as an exercise and very good it is too. Russell Grant the astrologer did a reading from it for me and gave me the chance of a very good job but more of that later.

One of the reasons why I stopped going to the astrology group in Quay Street was because one of the men kept staring at me very intensely. This went on for quite a few weeks and was very disturbing. On day he apologised to me and said "Please forgive me for staring but you really remind me of my favourite film star." Well naturally I primped my hair and licked my lips thinking he was comparing me to one of the glamorous female stars. My ego collapsed like a punctured balloon when he went on to say "Clint Eastwood", you look just like him." I bombarded family and friends to see if they could see any likeness – they couldn't and I felt a little bit better when comparing notes with Bill Roach he told me that the man had said the same thing to him.

Anyway, on to Russell Grant and Bill's chart. Leita Donn who was the Coronation Street Press Office and a work colleague was given an extra job to do. Russell Grant who was just on the edge of becoming very famous in England was doing a series of programmes for Granada and Leita was assigned to be his Press Officer. The Press Officers were responsible for writing press releases on the 'stars' of programmes, sending out publicity profiles and details of their programme. Leita was a very good P O and generated a good deal of publicity for her programmes as well as being mother confessor and guide to her 'stars'

Russell was very pleased with the work she was doing for him and said if she gave him her chart he would interpret it. Leita didn't have a chart and I think was not very interested in having a reading so she asked him if he could do mine, knowing that Bill. Who was a very special protégé of hers, had done a chart for me.

Russell was very kind and took my chart away coming in the following week with his interpretation. It was uncannily accurate and quite flattering. He told me that I had all the aspects of a good journalist, indeed stronger than some other journalists he knew. At the time I was working compiling the billings (or programme details) for all Granada programmes for the TV times. It could, I suppose, be classed on the very fringes of journalism but, as I told Russell not in much of a way. Russell then told me that a job was going to be advertised in Granada's press office – he didn't go into details of what it was only that it was tailor made for me but unless I applied I wouldn't get it, but if I applied it would be mine and I would be very happy in the post.

Working opposite me in the Press Office at the time was Mike Hill, the picture editor. Mike had joined Granada a year or so earlier coming from a similar job with TV Times. A lovely man, very good at his job which was arranging for photographic coverage of all Granada programmes for newspapers, magazines, overseas sales etc. Mike got on very well with everyone at work, but his wife and family missed the London scene and sadly he decided to go back to the TV Times. I worked quite closely with Mike because I had to deal with the TV Times on a daily basis and I was very sorry to hear he was leaving.

Mike's job was advertised and there was quite a lot of interest in it. The day before the closure date I spoke to my boss the chief Press Office, Norman Frisby. "Norman, who do you think would be ideal for the job of picture editor?" Norman answered, "You, but unless you apply for it you won't get it." I suddenly remember Russell Grant's word and sent in an application straight away.

Working in the Promotion, Presentation and Press Office had given me some of the skills needed for Picture Editor but I was nowhere near as qualified as some of the people from Fleet Street who had applied and I didn't think I stood a chance of getting the job.

Don Harker, the Executive Director of Granada's Press and Publicity, who was based in London, interviewed me. I was quite nervous, but the gentleman put me at my ease although I was certain that the job would be given to a more experienced person. I was short-listed with, as I expected, a very very experienced young man who was offered the job.

He was due to join Granada in a few weeks' time but straight away the men in the Dark Room and Photographic Dept, raised objections. They reasoned, quite rightly, that their jobs would be de-valued and didn't want such a high calibre person in charge.

I think also that Granada was having second thoughts about the appointment for the gentleman concerned insisted that he wanted his own office, secretary, car and other benefits. Mike Hill had had none of these and had been doing the job very well indeed, so I suppose it was decided to cancel the offer and happily they offered the job to me.

I was surprised, delighted and extremely pleased to be offered it and felt very grateful to Russell Grant for giving me the confidence to apply in the first place. and spent quite a good few happy years as Picture Editor before Granada did the 'cull' of staff and offered certain people the chance of redundancy. I was very happy in my work and had no intention of applying until my husband pointed out to me that my redundancy offer was very fair and so I applied and left in January 1990.

Whilst working as the billings clerk for the Granada edition of the TV Times I was still trying to find answers as to whether there was anything in fortune telling so I joined a group of other women who worked with me and we started going to see people who gave clairvoyant, palmistry and spiritual readings. Most of them were rubbish, especially with me because I wasn't going for any of the usual reasons – money, husband, health problems etc, so wasn't able to give them any hint of what my problem could be. I didn't have any reason for going other than being eager to find out if they could interpret the future.

One lady stood out above the others and was uncannily accurate in her predictions for me and the other women who went with me. The lady was quite old and lived in a small terraced typically 'Granny' type house. Unlike some of the other clairvoyants she was extremely reluctant to take any money from us but we insisted on giving her something.

Margaret one of the women I had worked with for a few years was quite giggly when she told us about her prediction. Apparently, she was going to meet a 'big huggy bear' of a man who would play an extremely important part in her life. This turn out to be completely true although she hadn't told us the full prediction and only told us in letters after she ran away to California with him a couple of years later. She only confided in one person, and the morning she left she arranged for this friend to hand out letters addressed to her boss at Granada, her husband, son and daughter and her friends.

She gave me some very good predictions too. Told me there was a young man (Paul our son) who was at a crossroads in his life (he was on the 'milk round at university) and that he would be offered some of the jobs. She said she could see a beautiful Rolls Royce with one job, I was not to influence him but if he took this he would be very successful. I knew that Paul had applied for quite a few jobs and had been offered three, one of which was at Rolls Royce in Derby. I didn't influence him, but he took this job and for a time had quite a good career there.

Another time she told me about a young man I would work closely with. This man had sandy hair going thin, and had the initials DB. I told her I used to work with David Black who had sandy hair but no longer worked with him and wasn't likely to do so again. She insisted that I would work extremely closely with this young man. She could see papers and photographs and a very close working relationship with him. There would be an awful tragedy associated with him and it would completely shock everyone when it.

Two years later I was given the job of Picture Editor and shortly afterwards Granada appointed a new, very talented young photographer called David Burroughs, who had sandy thinning hair, and with whom I would work very closely. I wrote earlier of the awful tragic circumstances of his death and all the people he knew were absolutely devastated when he died.

THE JEWEL IN THE CROWN

On the 26 January 1983 I left work a little later than normal, at about twenty to seven. I went to the car park where a Commissionaire stopped me and said, "I think you should get a photographer to the Bonded, it's on fire". I knew the Bonded Warehouse was very important: it was set up as the studio for THE JEWEL IN THE CROWN, replicating scenes that were first filmed in India and was full of props and costumes etc.

The only photographer on duty that night was David Burroughs who was assigned to film Johnny Hamp's THE GRUMBLEWEEDS- a comedy sketch programme. The red light was on and I knew it had to be something very important before anyone could interrupt the programme. Crossing my fingers that it was more than a fire in a wastepaper basket, I carefully opened the heavy doors and crawled along the floor trying to see David. He was across the studio and I somehow managed to get his attention and beckoned him to follow me out of the studio, he had a puzzled look on his face but when I told him "The Bonded is on fire", he needed no more telling and dashed out of the building.

He was just in time to film the fire from when it first took hold. The flames soared to over 50 feet high into the sky and could be seen all over the region. David got some magnificent film of the devastation.

It was never discovered what caused the blaze but luckily the cast and crew had left the building at 6 o'clock so no- one was injured but the building and contents were burned to the ground.

David and Stuart Derby were the photographers assigned to cover stills photography for filming of the JEWEL IN THE CROWN in India and England, taking it in turns to go to India with Stuart taking the first months of filming and David following towards the end.

It was a tragedy that all the props and costumes were burned because some of them were virtually irreplaceable and were needed for continuity purposes in the filming in England.

A team of people were sent out to antique shops, and junk shops in England and India to try and match the destroyed things. In Manchester people set to work to try to find still photographs of the items which were then used in the search for 'almost' exact items, and sent to antique shops, and junk shops in England and India to try and match the destroyed items. The christening shawl, which was an important prop near the end of the series when Barbie Bachelor was killed, was a particular problem. The delicate lace work depicting butterflies had taken months to make and a team of seamstresses had to work flat out to replace it in time for the filming.

Eventually the filming was finished, successfully as witnessed by the tributes given to the series.

I became quite friendly with David and his 'soon to be wife' Denise, who worked in Granada's Library and along with very many of their friends and colleagues, we went to their wedding. David was a brilliant photographer and was asked by a prestigious photographic society to submit some of his work so that he could be considered as a member. David was accepted but very sadly, it was as a posthumous member because almost exactly one year after his marriage David died. It was very sudden and unexpected. David appeared to be a very fit young man; indeed, he had run the Manchester Marathon not long before he was taken ill. David complained of a very bad back, but everyone thought this was the result of carrying around some heavy camera equipment.

He came into work one day and obviously in a great deal of pain he said "I don't know Joan, I think I've had it" Foolishly as it happened I told him "Look, David, I know what you're thinking but if it was cancer you wouldn't be in such pain when you've only just been taken ill."   But it was cancer, pancreatic cancer, which is usually fatal and within about six weeks David had died, in a very painful way. Everyone who knew him was devastated and couldn't believe it had happened to such a very likeable and talented young man.

I had many fond memories of him one I remembered with some amusement.   During the filming of George Orwell's "The Road to 1984, which starred one of the Fox brothers, we decided to have a major photo call (I believe they are called photo shoots now) in the open cast coal mine which featured in some of the scenes. David was waiting for a new car to be delivered from the Continent because you could get a good bargain by buying one there. He asked if I could give him a life in my Spitfire.

It was a blistering hot day when we set off, in my newly washed car, with the hood down and the pair of us wearing beanie hats. We drove through the mine to the accompanying shouts of encouragement and whistles from the working miners, looking like a real pair of wallies.

It was a very successful call because most of the major newspaper journalists and photographers were there.   The actual scene they were filming was George Orwell standing on top of a slagheap watching dozens of people scrambling among the coal dust looking for small pieces of coal. After this scene it was decided to take extra publicity shots of David Fox. We set up a suitable place for the photographers to take this and because the sun was so fierce, I started to position a silver umbrella so that we could diffuse the glare.

One of the electricians, a union shop steward from the ETU (electrical trades union) came over to me, as I thought, for a chat.

"What are you doing, Joan" he said.

"Oh, positioning this brolly to get better pictures."

"Oh no, you're not" he said, "That's an electricians' job".

I thought he was joking until I saw his face. He was deadly serious.

"Okay that's all right with me," I said "but you can't have this umbrella it's the photographic dept property. We need to have a diffused photograph so what are you going to do. You'll have to turn the sun off if lighting is your job." We glared at each other until we both saw the funny side of the situation and burst out laughing. "Here, I said have a toffee." This diffused the demarcation between photographers and electrician jobs, for a time.

Everyone had a good laugh, we got a great deal of press coverage and David and I set off home. I dropped David off at his house but when I got home Leo, my husband looked at me in disgust. The car and me were covered from head to foot, or boot to bumper with thick black dirt. Leo got a hosepipe and sluiced the car down I only just managed to stop him turning the water on to me by rushing into the shower, and the gutters outside our house ran down for ages with thick black coal dust.

Figure 23 The spectacular fire at Granada's Bonded Warehouse, Photograph taken by David Burroughs

FIFTEEN MINUTES OF FAME

I think it was Andy Warhol who predicted that in the future everyone would have 15 minutes of fame. Well I suppose you can say that I have had some of mine, but as usual things didn't always go to plan.

In the 1970's Gordon Burns presented a local programme, which set out to measure stress and find out which of the different kinds of relaxation was the most effective. There were four or five categories: cup of tea, biofeedback, hypnotism, Yoga and I think here was another, which I don't remember.

Penderil Reed (whose Christian name was handed down through the family and was given to the first born irrespective of sex) was the Yoga teacher for the weekly sessions, which were provided by Granada during our lunch break. Penderil taught Iyenga Yoga and was indeed very inspiring and wonderful teacher. Not only did she have success in streamlining figures, soothing nerves but also helped ease bad backs.

The producer of a programme about stress approached Penderil and asked if she would be willing to take someone through Yoga postures on the programme. For my sins Penderil asked me to be her guinea pig.

Dressed in my usual well-worn leotard Penderil and I did warming up exercises together and then she went through the poses she intended to use on the programme. So far so good. I was then fitted with electrodes, similar, or may be they were the same, as those used to test heartbeats. Then we had the rehearsal... Penderil took me through Asanders, or poses, the Sanskrit names of which I can't spell or remember but which involved standing stretches, shoulder lifts, etc into which I put good deal of effort; suddenly the studio was plunged into darkness all the lights had fused. Quickly the control room switched to emergency lighting whilst they looked for the problem. They soon found it...it was me, apparently, or so they said, my electrodes hadn't been placed properly, but considering that I was being very energetic and I have a strange heartbeat I wonder if that was the reason.

Very soon everything went back to normal, we did the exercises then I lay down on the yoga mat whilst Mrs Reed took me through the breathing and relaxing exercises. These were a very popular part of the lessons at work, indeed so relaxing were they that often-muffled snores would break the silence, I don't know if I snored on the programme but it was then recorded without a hitch. They found that, believe it or not, a cup of tea proved the winner, with bio- feedback next and Yoga the third. However, considering I was the only person to do strenuous exercises I didn't think I, or Yoga did too badly.

Figure 24 Me with Penderil Reed and Gordon Burn

Then shortly after this The Krypton factor producers decided to make the assault course more difficult and decided to film this at the army assault course at Holcombe Brook near Bury. Because it was going to be more strenuous it was decided to take people of varying standards of fitness and age and give out handicaps. I think it was decided that as I was older than most of the people who had 'volunteered' to take part in the experiment, and because they knew I had done Yoga and, although completely unathletic, was probably reasonably fit I was asked to take part.

Although the army sergeant in charge of the exercise was rather doubtful about letting me take part because I had never done vigorous exercise in my life, and was in my forties, I was given a tracksuit and a very good handicap, and set off, way before the signal was given for anyone else to start.

I jogged along and went through some of the sections but when it came to balancing along logs I kept falling off and had to start over and over again. In the end they told me to carry on anyway, I was all right going under the nets in muddy water then another problem – I had to climb up a wall, jumping up to try to get a handhold and then clamber up. I couldn't do it and eventually I had two soldiers pushing me up by my behind and another two at the top helping me up. The zip line though was easy and although I was once again splattered with water at the end I got through and staggered to the finishing line – well behind the athletic types who had started long after me.

I dried myself off and changed into shorts and t-shirt then joined my friends who were sunbathing on the grass and watching the filming. Jeremy Fox, one of the researchers came up to me and said "Nick (the producer) has got a problem, one of the 'volunteers 'has refused to do the next lap and Nick wonders if you would run it again because you look less knackered than the others" – which was probably true because I hadn't over-exerted myself as the athletic types had done. Believing he was joking I said, "Yes, of course I'll do it." And settled down to sunbathe with my friends.

Minutes later Jeremy came back rather flustered: "Come on Joan, get your track suit on we are all waiting for you".

"But, but" I said, "I thought you were joking".

"I wasn't" said Jeremy "And you'll have to do it now they are all waiting for you.

In a rather confused state, I set off again with, I think an even bigger handicap this time. I had the same problems as before and the same triumphs and this time my legs turned to jelly near the end but I somehow managed to finish. Afterwards I got a very nice 'thank you' letter from Nick Turnbull, the producer, expressing his surprise that a mere weak woman had managed to do the course twice consecutively…

I think now I should let my husband get in on the act for his five minutes of fame. ITV were looking, apparently unsuccessfully, for a female Avenger. Leo said to me one night that he thought Joanna Lumley would be ideal for this.

A friend at work, Leita Donn, was the press officer for Coronation Street and had become good friends with Joanna when she had appeared in Coronation Street as the love interest for Ken Barlow. The next day I mentioned to her what Leo had said and she looked very thoughtful and said she thought that was a good idea.

That evening Leita phoned Joanna who said she quite fancied the idea and would get her agent on to the job. Then to our surprise weeks later we received this rather splendid photograph from Joanna.

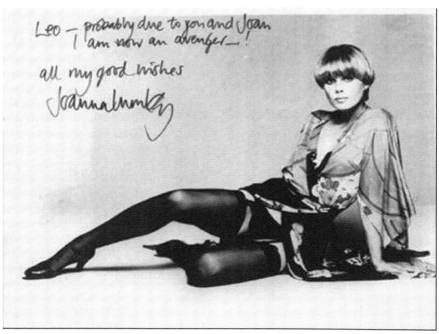

Figure 25 Joanna Lumley dedication

NORWEGIAN CROWN

For years I kept asking Leo if we could go on a cruise. He kept telling me that he thought he would be bored and that he didn't think there would be much to do on board ship. He was completely wrong on both scores. Then we saw an advert for a cruise leaving in the next month. It was advertised as 'Two for one' and seemed to be a good bargain. Reluctantly Leo agreed to take a chance and told me to book it. He was even more sceptical when he saw a photograph of the cabin we would be getting. "I'll believe that when I see it," he said.

We had a flight to Miami where we were to stay for one night and then would be taken to the ship. After a rather enjoyable overnight stay in the hotel we sat down in the foyer waiting for transport to the ship. Waiting with us were two other couples who introduced themselves and we talked about the cruise and became quite friendly in the 20 minutes or so we stood waiting. Jean, one of the ladies walked over to our suitcases and, rather rudely I thought, proceeded to examine the labels. "Oh" she said, "You are on the same deck and in similar cabins to us but you are Port and we are Starboard. "

The talk then got around to dining; the other couple and ourselves had been allocated table numbers, Jean and Brian had no number. Jean said "Wouldn't it be nice if we could all share the same table? Did you say your number was 12?" I jokingly replied that she wouldn't be able to join us because we were sitting with the Captain". I thought she looked a little put out by this and hoped she hadn't taken me seriously.

We had booked a last minute 'two for one' deal and were very pleasantly surprised when we saw our cabin. We had expected a poky little room but this was spacious with a large bow shaped window along one end with a fitted seat in front of it. Very nice indeed.

Once settled in we went for a walk on deck and were standing at the rails talking to another couple when the four people from the hotel, who were two decks up, shouted something to us. It sounded something like dinner and a table. We excused ourselves to our new friends and went looking for them to find out what they had said but couldn't find them.

Our allocated table was set in the middle of the room on a small platform, in a most pleasant position. Four American couples were already seated when we arrived. They were very friendly and greeted us with "Hi, I'm Hank, this is Mildred" and so on round the table.

"Which part do you hail from" said Hank.

"Manchester, England" we replied.

"Gee Manchester, we have kinfolk in Chester, name of Baker, you probably know them". We tried not to smile when we replied that we didn't know many people from Chester.

As we spoke, I noticed the headwaiter with another couple hovering around. He came up to us and said, "I'm afraid you are on the wrong table". Surprised we showed him our form with the table number. "No this is table 12 our table." we replied. Puzzled he went back to his desk and came back saying, "Oh, it seems your friends have asked for you to be moved to their table. If you follow the waiter he will show you the way." Meekly we followed but with hindsight should have strongly objected but as it was our first proper cruise we didn't want to make a fuss.

We were escorted out of the main dining room into a small annexe which contained two tables for 10 one table for 6 and a very small table which was obviously intended for two but which had two extra chairs round it. Jean and Brian, the couple from the hotel, were already seated. Needless to say they were in the only seats that faced into the room. I sat facing a blank screen and Brian, and Leo faced a blank wall and Jean, Leo's seat was part way into the aisle. The screen facing me was hiding the kitchen entrance and a steady stream of waiters rushed past jostling Leo throughout our meals, not very pleasant seats.

"What's going on" we asked "Oh its all right" said Jean offhandedly. "We asked for you to be put on our table." "Well, thanks very much" I said very annoyed. No, to be truthful we were not annoyed we were absolutely furious at such high-handed behaviour. "But why? We had a lovely table with very friendly Americans and were just thrown off," we replied trying our best not to show how annoyed we were. "Oh this is a nice table too, you'll be better off here with people you know." Fine, on the basis of a short conversation whilst waiting for transport we were now bosom pals.

"What happened to your other friends? I thought you'd be sharing with them", we asked through gritted teeth. "Well, said Jean, "we all came down to see where our tables were and they said they were perfectly happy with the table they had been allocated so didn't want to move. That's why we asked for you to be put with us." Leo and I just stared at one another; we'd never before heard such barefaced cheek. There didn't, however, seem to be much we could do, we knew the ship was full, so all we could do was try and make the best of it.

Unfortunately, our waiter had spent just three weeks as a bus boy (the assistant who brings water and takes the dirty plates away) when he was promoted. This was his first week as a waiter and it certainly showed. A very large Jamaican, over friendly to the point of nausea and very false, he gave off an air of menace. He had a strong accent, which was hard to understand, but for seven days at every meal he made sure we understood the same rehearsed speech. With the first course it was "Dis my first week as waiter. Ver important I get good reference at end of week. You give me good reference. I good waiter, yes? (Well actually no). I need job." With the next course it was "Me have pretty little wife and three babies in Kingston. I need money to keep them. You give me tips at end of holiday. You give me big tips, then I very happy man." With the sweet course came "One day I get my own place, a fancy restaurant. I save for it. If you give me good tips then I get soon maybe in 12 months."

Although we found this performance quite funny at first, it became so irritating we all felt like walking out. He was sarcastic and quite rude to Jean and me. He took our orders in a mocking singsong little child's voice, making fun of us. He missed our courses and brought the wrong dishes at times. We knew very well though that he was quite capable of spitting in our soup or doing something obscene to our steaks if we complained so we just smiled weakly and kept quiet.

After seething quietly for a few days about the high-handed manner our companions had changed the table, Leo spoke quietly to the Maitre d' pointing out he should make sure both couples wanted to move. He nodded as though he understood but…that evening he came to our table and very undiplomatically said, "I believe you don't like the people on this table and would like to move. I'm very sorry but all the tables are full." We were absolutely horrified at his attitude and protested that we liked the people on the table but thought he should have asked our permission before moving us.

Jean and Brian were both annoyed thinking that we had taken a personal dislike to them and were very upset and nothing we said could alter the strained atmosphere. For the next two nights they didn't come down to dinner and apparently ate their meals in the buffet café. This upset us too and Leo went and had a quiet word with them explaining that in no way had we said, or implied that we didn't like them, just that the Maitre d' should speak to both parties before changing tables,

Jean and Brian were a pleasant enough couple and under different circumstances we would probably have been quite good friends, but Leo and I couldn't get over our resentment about what they had done and although the atmosphere was amicable enough after this, we couldn't relax with them. It turned out to be a fantastic holiday, which we enjoyed very much except for the tension at mealtimes.

OOPS

Recently I informed Paul, our son, that I had decided I had reached an age when I could be eccentric and be forgiven for getting up to all sorts of stupid tricks. Paul looked at me very seriously and said, "I've got some bad news for you mum". "Oh", said I, "what is wrong." He replied, "You've always been eccentric, what's new?"

I asked him to explain this insult to his old mother and he said two words "Kettle and tea bags amongst other things."

Well the kettle incident is easily explained away. Electric kettles were in their infancy when we got a fine stainless steel one. Understandably, not being used to it I forgot and put it on the gas hob where the bottom got burnt out.

The tea bags…well I had a rather flattering suntan after having the usual two weeks in the sun. Asking a friend at work if she had any ideas of keep brown a little bit longer, she replied, "Rub tea leaves all over and it will keep the tan going."

Not a good idea, the leaves just dropped off and made a mess so I went to bed and thought that wasn't a very good idea. Early in the morning I woke – I quite often have good ideas when I first wake up and I thought this was inspired. Tea bags, that's the answer. Putting newspaper on the floor and wetting two tea bags I stood in the middle of the kitchen at about 6 o'clock in the morning, half naked and rubbed the bags over my face and arms. I then got replacement bags, wet them, and getting more into the swing of the thing started to do a war dance with appropriate Indian whooping chants while rubbing the bags all over my body.

I happened to glance up just as I was in full war chant to see a face pressed against the kitchen window, it was pressed so close that it looked as though the man was wearing a stocking mask. It was the dustman. Shouting an apologetic "sorry" I flung myself and tea bags on to the newspaper covered floor and lay there until I thought it safe to appear again. I don't remember seeing this dustman again, but I may have been mistaken because they usually disappeared rather quickly when I appeared.

On another occasion whilst walking through fields at Deya in Majorca, the fields disappeared, and we came to a rubbish tip and then open countryside. We seemed to be lost. Then a group of people came walking towards us, obviously they knew where the lane led and I, trying to be funny said, "Doctor Livingstone, I presume". To me this seemed quite a good way of introducing ourselves as we asked for directions. Looking puzzled and gazing at us with suspicion the group replied, as one, "Nicht Verstehen", obviously they were German and when we realised this tried to make them think we had just been asking for directions. They pointed the way and we carried on until we reached a rather ancient boat, we sat down for a rest and then some other people came and we were given Cuba Libras, and asked for a stupidly small amount of money. The boat set sail, (we were all rather merry for the Captain was very generous with his drinks); we knew not where we were going but finally landed in a beautiful little port, which we found out later, was Porter Soller.

Again, we came out of a cinema that was rather out of the way for us and had just started looking in an estate agents window when a young couple came up to us and seemed to know us very well, and started talking about all sort of things. Leo and I looked at each other, obviously neither of us knew who the couple were, and I tried to surreptitiously find out who they were by asking some rather inane questions. I then asked them if they were still living in the same house. They looked rather shocked and said "Yes, next door but two to you, didn't you recognise us?" Being embarrassed and not knowing what to say I blurted out "Oh, we didn't recognise you with your clothes on" – this being a reference to the fact that Trisha next door and this lady and I used to iron in our bikinis when the weather was fine…They took the explanation in good part, however, and have pulled our legs about it ever since. After all they had been our neighbours for only about 6 years.

I must have got quite a reputation with the dustmen in our area. Leo and I decided to buy a new mattress for one of our beds. The old one was leaning up in the hall waiting for us to find some way of getting rid of it. Next time the dustmen came to empty our bins. I called one of them over and said. "Excuse me but if I give you some money will..." he didn't let me finish but said very eagerly "Yes, "Yes". When I finished off with... "Move a mattress for me" he looked quite crestfallen. Probably he'd watched too many TV plays where the lady of the house fancies a workman!!

Quite naturally our marriage hasn't always been smooth sailing, we have had our moments. After the war when factories were moving over from 'Utility' furniture to the more substantial kind. (Personally I have always quite liked the Utility style) my mother bought a new dining room suite: four chairs, table and sideboard. The chairs and table were all right but the sideboard...well my mother hated it as soon as she got it home but was stuck with it until... When we moved into our first house Mam saw a perfect way to demonstrate her undoubted generosity and also get rid of the suite at the same time. She donated it to us. I hated it as well but it served its purpose for we were badly in need of furniture at the time. Eventually we decided to buy a rather nice oval table and chairs and matching wall cupboards and got rid of the table and chairs given by Mam. The sideboard was more difficult to cope with; it was mahogany (perhaps) veneer with thick bulbous feet and two heavy doors at the sides. Leo put it in the hall until ready to break it up and take it to the tip. It was so big that it had to go against the front door and that could only open enough to give a whispered instruction to any visitor to "go round the side". I kept asking Leo to get rid of it and he kept saying "I'll do it tomorrow", well everyone knows tomorrow never comes.

It then got to just a couple of weeks before Christmas and I was anxious to get the house all nice and decorated 'cos Leo's mother was coming for Christmas dinner. The flipping sideboard was giving me nightmares; I couldn't think of anything else it was driving me mad, until one day I snapped. Pushing and shoving the thing I got it down the hall and into the kitchen where with a strength I didn't know I possessed I bumped it over the step and onto the path.

I still don't know how I managed to wrench the doors off their hinges, but I did, and flung them onto the path.   Then grabbing a pickaxe from the shed I proceeded to lob it onto the top of the sideboard, pulling and tugging at the wood and flinging the bits on the path. Paul, our son was about 7 or 8 at the time and he and his pals stood wide-eyed. They sent a scout out to tell their other pals, "Come quick, Mrs Riley has gone crazy and is breaking up their furniture with a pickaxe". Once demolished, I piled the bits of wood neatly at the side of the house and went inside. To say husband Leo was not amused was a vast understatement, he was livid. I was called a "bad-tempered b...." and sent to Coventry.

Christmas, and Leo's mum came to dinner, and all conversation from Leo was directed through her – it was not a very 'merry' Christmas.

However, two good things seemingly came from this. Paul went up in the world with his friends. They were scared to upset his "mad" mother, especially when she had access to an axe. And come New Year, Leo relented and took the wood to the tip. He came back and rather sheepishly said "Good job you broke the sideboard up: it had wood worm."

When I was working in Gra's press office I was friendly with Monica a reporter on the Liverpool Echo. Her husband had researched and written books on reincarnation and later on appeared on TV discussing his findings.

They invited my O/H and me to their house and Monica's husband regressed me back first to my first day at school when I wet my knickers and stood in a pool of water, then to the 16th century as a drummer boy in a Scottish Regiment.

Before we went my O/H was very sceptical and called it a load of rubbish but he agreed to take me and would watch and, I suppose say it was rubbish.

Afterwards I wasn't really convinced because I just felt very relaxed and said things that came into my head, but Leo was absolutely amazed. He said he saw me change into a frightened child and then into a stroppy lad.

The gentleman told us that he had regressed a group of people who were in some way connected in this life and surprisingly they all told the same story of their deaths – they were in something like a church and were burned to death. He researched this and discovered that a large number of people sought refuge in a church in York, the church was set alight and the people all perished.

A very interesting couple but unfortunately it was quite some time ago and I have forgotten most of the details.

Figure 26 The Photo Finish

Epilogue

Leo and I were married in August 1952.

Then In 2012 when to our complete astonishment, we received a lovely Diamond Anniversary card from Her Majesty The Queen. We hadn't realised that you receive a card on the 60th anniversary and at first thought it was because The Queen was celebrating her Diamond Anniversaries as well.

This picture of the whole family was taken on our anniversary at the Hare and Hounds in Timperley, near Manchester:

Figure 27 The Bond and Riley Family in 2013

Present from left to right are:
Gill Riley, Joan Riley (Me), Leo Riley, Paul Riley, Eric Bond, Anne Bond, Alan and Jean Bond, Malcolm and Doreen Bond. Centre stage is The Queen's photograph on the front of the card she sent to us.

Paul (my son) was awarded his PhD in 2014 (age 60!) and his wife Gill an MBE in in the same year....An achievement coming from my single parent Mum.

DNA test

In 2018, I did one of the Ancestry DNA tests to find out who I am related to - later that year, Paul had an Email from a TV production company saying that I am related to someone in Coronation Street. They didn't disclose the name.

CRUISING

In later life, Leo and I have taken to cruising - the things one does on ships not in toilets!
Last year in 2018 on the Navigator of the Seas, my son Paul always the engineer, entered a competition to build a boat from scrap found around the ship, this is him being interviewed before the event.

Figure 28 Paul in 2018 entering a boat building competition

Paul and another man made the boat with the help of friends we had made as we took advantage of the goodies and drinks available in the Concierge lounge. Everyone joined in scavenging around the ship for bottles, steel coat hangers, crayons. Concierge Patricia gave us a small Union Jack, paper clips, and elastic bands, which were used to power the ship, Gill made a model of Patricia which when fastened to the prow she kindly christened with the a small bottle of pop. Launching the Queen Mary, it was not, but very enjoyable anyway. When the model's wig came off in the swimming pool, the officer in charge had everyone laughing when he joked that Patricia was looking very butch. Friends from Texas videoed the whole scene and kindly sent it to us when we got home, it brought back lovely memories. We have been to a lot of lovely places and had fantastic times on cruises, mostly on P & O, Celebrity and Royal Caribbean cruises. Happy days.

And finally, our other pastime is Warner Leisure Centres. Here is Leo and I Christmas 2018 at Alvaston.

Figure 29 Leo and Joan at Alvaston Hotel Cheshire Christmas 2018

Printed in Great Britain
by Amazon

59895557R00133